ECONOMIC AND SOCIAL COMMISSION FOR ASIA AND THE PACIFIC

STATISTICAL PROFILES

WOMEN IN SAMOA

A COUNTRY PROFILE

UNITED NATIONS
New York, 1997

ST/ESCAP/1701

UNITED NATIONS PUBLICATION

Sales No. E.97.II.F.20

ISBN 92-1-119757-0

This profile has been issued without formal editing.

The profile has been prepared under the project BK-X20-3-214 Improving Statistics on Women in the ESCAP Region.

FOREWORD

The call for the development of statistics and indicators on the situation of women has for some time been voiced in various global and regional forums. It was first recommended by the World Plan of Action for the Implementation of the Objectives of the International Women's Year, adopted in 1975. The recommendations of the World Plan of Action were reaffirmed and elaborated in the Programme of Action for the Second Half of the United Nations Decade for Women. The Economic and Social Commission for Asia and the Pacific on various occasions, stressing the importance of social and human development, has recognized the need for improved statistics and indicators on women. It has noted that better indicators were required to monitor the situation of women and to assess the effectiveness of strategies and programmes designed to address priority gender issues.

The secretariat initiated the project on improving statistics on women in the ESCAP region in 1994. The project aims to support Governments in their efforts to promote the full integration of women in development and improve their status in line with the Nairobi Forward-looking Strategies for the Advancement of Women. The project has been implemented by the Economic and Social Commission for Asia and the Pacific (ESCAP) through its subprogramme on statistics, with funding assistance from the Government of the Netherlands.

As a major component of its activities the project commissioned experts from 19 countries in the region to prepare country profiles on the situation of women and men in the family, at work, and in public life by analysing available statistical data and information. The profiles are intended to highlight the areas where action is needed, and to raise the consciousness of the readers about issues concerning women and men. The 19 countries are Bangladesh, China, India, Indonesia, Islamic Republic of Iran, Japan, Nepal, Pakistan, Philippines, Republic of Korea, Sri Lanka, and Thailand in Asia; and Cook Islands, Fiji, Papua New Guinea, Samoa, Solomon Islands, Tonga, and Vanuatu in the Pacific.

The secretariat hosted two meetings each in Asia and in the Pacific as part of the project activities. In the first meeting, the experts discussed and agreed on the structure, format, and contents of the country profiles based on guidelines prepared by the secretariat through Ms C.N. Ericta, consultant. The second meeting was a workshop to review the draft profiles. Participants in the workshop included the country experts and invited representatives from national statistical offices of Brunei Darussalam, Hong Kong, Lao People's Democratic Republic, Mongolia, and Viet Nam in Asia; Marshall Islands, Tuvalu, and Vanuatu in the Pacific; and United Nations organizations, specialized agencies, and international organizations.

The original draft of the present profile, *Women in Samoa,* was prepared by Ms Tina Tau'asosi, Foreign Affairs Officer of the Ministry of Foreign Affairs. It was technically edited and modified by the ESCAP secretariat with the assistance of Mr S. Selvaratnam, consultant. The profiles express the views of the authors and not necessarily those of the secretariat.

I wish to express my sincere appreciation to the Government of the Netherlands for its generous financial support, which enabled the secretariat to implement the project.

Adrianus Mooy
Executive Secretary

The call for the development of statistics and indicators on the situation of women has for some time been voiced in various global and regional forums. It was first recommended by the World Plan of Action for the implementation of the Objectives of the International Women's Year, adopted in 1975. The recommendations of the World Plan of Action were reaffirmed and elaborated in the Programme of Action for the Second Half of the United Nations Decade for Women. The Economic and Social Commission for Asia and the Pacific has, on various occasions, stressing the importance of social and human development, has recognized the need for improved statistics and indicators on women. It has noted that better indicators were required to monitor the situation of women and to assess the effectiveness of strategies and programmes designed to address priority gender issues.

The secretariat initiated the project on improving statistics on women in the ESCAP region in 1994. The project aims to support Governments in their efforts to promote the full integration of women in development and improve their status in line with the Nairobi Forward-looking Strategies for the Advancement of Women. The project has been implemented by the Economic and Social Commission for Asia and the Pacific (ESCAP) through its subprogramme on statistics, with funding assistance from the Government of the Netherlands.

As a major component of its activities the project commissioned experts from 19 countries in the region to prepare country profiles on the situation of women and men in the family, at work, and in public life by analysing available statistical data and information. The profiles are intended to highlight the areas where action is needed, and to raise the consciousness of the readers about issues concerning women and men. The 19 countries are Bangladesh, China, India, Indonesia, Islamic Republic of Iran, Japan, Nepal, Pakistan, Philippines, Republic of Korea, Sri Lanka, and Thailand in Asia; and Cook Islands, Fiji, Papua New Guinea, Samoa, Solomon Islands, Tonga, and Vanuatu in the Pacific.

The secretariat hosted two meetings each in Asia and in the Pacific as part of the project activities. In the first meeting, the experts discussed and agreed on the structure, format, and contents of the country profile, based on guidelines prepared by the secretariat through Ms C.N. Dutta, consultant. The second meeting was a workshop to review the draft profiles. Participants in the workshop included the country experts and invited representatives from national statistical offices of Brunei Darussalam, Hong Kong, Lao People's Democratic Republic, Mongolia, and Viet Nam in Asia; Marshall Islands, Tuvalu, and Vanuatu in the Pacific; and United Nations organizations, specialized agencies, and international organizations.

The original draft of the present profile, Women in Samoa, was prepared by Ms Tina Fa'u Sioa, Foreign Affairs Officer of the Ministry of Foreign Affairs. It was technically edited and modified by the ESCAP secretariat with the assistance of Mr S. Selvaratnam, consultant. The profiles express the views of the authors and not necessarily those of the secretariat.

I wish to express my sincere appreciation to the Government of the Netherlands for its generous financial support, which enabled the secretariat to implement the project.

Adrianus Mooy
Executive Secretary

CONTENTS

LIST OF TEXT TABLES

LIST OF TEXT TABLES *(Continued)*

LIST OF FIGURES

LIST OF STATISTICAL TABLES

PART I:
DESCRIPTIVE ANALYSIS

INTRODUCTION

In Samoa, as in most small island countries of the Pacific, women have traditionally played the role of homemakers. However, in recent decades women have been increasingly participating in various facets of socio-economic life, playing an active role, particularly in agriculture, commerce and trade, health, education and community services. For instance, women have a central role in health as caretakers of the family and village health and sanitation through the Women's Committees. Each community has a women's committee which is responsible for the promotion of village health and sanitation by carrying out inspections and working closely with health authorities.

Recognizing the vital contribution that women can and should make to national development, the Government had created a Ministry of Women's Affairs, which is responsible for the formulation and implementation of programmes and projects for enhancing the social and economic status of women in the country. The Government has also appointed a Women's Advisory Committee to advise the Minister for Women's Affairs on matters of interest or concern to women and women's committees and organizations. The Advisory Committee also assists the Ministry in carrying out the government's policies in regard to the work of women and women's organizations.

At present, there are more than 50 non-governmental women's organizations registered with the Ministry of Women's Affairs. Of these, two are large umbrella organizations: the National Council of Women with over 2,000 individual members; and the Women's Development Committee with over 6,000 individual members. The non-governmental women's organizations largely comprise health committees, community development groups, sports groups, church-related groups, educational groups, alumni associations, fund-raising groups, and internationally affiliated groups. All these groups participate in the relevant activities and projects implemented by the Ministry of Women's Affairs.

Despite the active intervention of the government and non-governmental organizations, the formulation of comprehensive plans and programmes for the betterment of Samoan women is handicapped to a considerable extent by the lack of reliable and up-to-date statistical data and information relating to various issues and concerns affecting women. The present profile attempts to bring together the available data with a view to highlighting gaps and deficiencies in existing data and knowledge about women in Samoa. It is hoped that the profile would serve as a basis for appropriate initiatives and actions to improve and strengthen the data bases on various aspects of women's concerns in the country.

A. HIGHLIGHTS

The setting

1.   Samoa, a Polynesian small-island nation in the South Pacific, comprises two large islands of Savaii and Upolu, and two small islands of Manonu and Apolima. The total land area of 2,934 square kilometres is almost entirely distributed between Savaii (1,820 square kilometres) and Upolu (1,110 square kilometres).

2.   The climate is tropical with temperatures generally ranging from 20°C to 30°C. Tropical cyclones, some very destructive, have occurred frequently in recent years.

3.   After over a century of foreign suzerainty, Samoa became an independent nation on 1 January 1962. Since then, the islands have been governed under a parliamentary system. The national legislative assembly (Fono) comprises 47 members of whom 45 were until 1990 elected by *matai* suffrage. Universal suffrage introduced in 1990 granted voting rights to all adults aged 21 years and over.

4.   The total population of the country, as enumerated at the latest census held in November 1991, was 161,298 of which about 72 per cent resided in Upolu, where the population of Apia, the capital, totalled 34,126 persons.

5. The indigenous people of Samoa are Polynesian and account for 98 per cent of the total population. The essential unit of the traditional social system is the *aiga* or extended family which is headed by a *matai* or chief chosen by consensus of family members. Christianity is the religion of the overwhelming majority of the people.

6. Samoa is classified among the least developed countries of the world. The national economy is heavily dependent on agriculture, forestry and fisheries. Traditional subsistence agriculture comprises 80 per cent of the area under cultivation and contributes to a substantial proportion of the nation's gross domestic products.

7. Compared to most Pacific developing countries, Samoa's social indicators are generally favourable with very high proportions of children attending school, and the health status of the people in terms of morbidity and mortality improving rapidly over the past few decades.

Women's profile

1. Males have outnumbered females in the total population at every census count. In 1991, there were about 110 males for every 100 females or about 91 females per 100 males in the country. The preponderance of males in the total population is attributed to a male-favoured sex ratio at birth, higher female than male mortality in the past, and substantial underenumeration of females at the censuses.

2. The population of Samoa is young, in that 53.6 per cent of males and 52.7 per cent of females were below 20 years of age. The proportionate share of children aged 0-14 years in the total population was about the same for both males and females.

3. Among persons aged 15 years and over, 54 per cent of females as against 47 per cent of males were married. The incidence of widowhood as well as divorce or separation was considerably higher among females than males.

4. In recent years, women have constituted an increasing proportion among those emigrating from the country. About 19 per cent of female emigrants and 21 per cent of male emigrants reported employment as the main reason for leaving the country.

5. Available data show that there have been improvements in school participation rates between 1981 and 1991 and that these rates were significantly higher for females than males. At the 1991 census, 85 per cent of females and 84 per cent of males aged 5-19 years were reported being in full-time education.

Women in family life

1. There is a strong tendency among young persons to refrain from early marriage but enter into marital union at a later stage. The 1991 Population Census reported that 94.1 per cent of females at ages 15-19 and 59.4 per cent at ages 20-24 remained single. The mean age at marriage was 28.3 years for males and 24.3 years for females.

2. Estimates based on census data indicate that the total fertility rate declined from 6.7 in 1981 to 4.7 in 1991. Nevertheless, the current fertility rate is considered high in comparison with most other Polynesian island countries.

3. Total number of contraceptors declined from 6,243 in 1991 to 5,568 in 1992. Nearly 43 per cent of family planning acceptors use Depo Provera, while another 23 per cent use oral pills.

4. The relatively high fertility rates place a considerable health burden on women and children. Despite easy availability of maternal and child health services, only about 55 per cent of pregnant women attended antenatal clinics in 1992. A substantial number of birth deliveries were reported taking place at home and being assisted by untrained traditional birth attendants.

5. Maternal mortality rate is currently estimated at 50 per 100,000 live births. Infant mortality rate is estimated to have declined from 158 per 1,000 births in 1950-1955 to 64 in 1990-1995. The rapid decline in infant mortality rate has largely been due to the success of the expanded programme of immunization.

6. Life expectancy at birth has shown considerable improvement over the past four decades. In 1990-1995, life expectancy of 69.2 years for females was significantly higher than the 65.9 years estimated for males.

7. As noted earlier, incidence of marital disruption through widowhood or divorce/separation is higher among females than males. The higher life expectancy of females, compared with males, is an important factor contributing to higher rate of widowhood among females. Another reason is the greater chance of remarriage for widowed males, compared with widowed females.

8. According to the 1991 census, only 16.5 per cent of the households in the country were headed by females. The vast majority of female household heads were either widowed, single, or separated/divorced.

Women in economic life

1. Although women contribute very significantly to economic production, their participation in economic activity has been considerably underreported for various reasons. According to the 1991 census of population, only about 40 per cent of females aged 15 years and over were reported being economically active, while the corresponding proportion among males was 77 per cent. The participation rates for males were also higher than the corresponding female rates at all ages.

2. Nearly 37 per cent of employed females and 33 per cent of employed males were in paid employment. The majority of employed males (67 per cent) and females (63 per cent) worked primarily to grow, gather or catch food.

3. The vast majority of employed females (66.4 per cent) as well as employed males (72.7 per cent) were engaged in agriculture, forestry and fishing sectors. A higher proportion among females (18.7 per cent) compared with males (10.5 per cent) was employed in community, social and personal services.

4. The occupational distribution of the employed persons more or less reflects their indus-

trial attachment pattern; 64.4 per cent among females and 70.5 per cent among males were employed as agricultural or fishing workers. A significantly higher proportion of females than males was engaged as senior officials, professional technicians and clerks.

5. The largest proportions of employed males (66.8 per cent) and females (65.0 per cent) were unpaid family workers; only about 32 per cent of employed females as against 26 per cent of employed males were in paid employment.

6. According to the 1991 population census, female unemployment rate of 3.1 per cent was twice the rate of 1.5 per cent for males. Females aged 15-19 years experienced the highest unemployment rate of 11.3 per cent.

7. The 1981 Census of Agriculture revealed that women constituted only 2.4 per cent of all agricultural operators (persons who exercise management control over the operation of an agricultural holding) in the country.

8. A 1991 ad hoc survey showed that more females than males were engaged in urban informal economic activities such as selling vegetables, fruits, root crops, handicraft items and imported commodities such as garments, perfumes and footwear.

9. In 1991, females constituted approximately 41 per cent of the private sector employees in Samoa. In that year, of the 2,862 private sector employers, only 148 or 5.2 per cent were women.

10. Among the 38,687 persons aged 15 years and over reported not economically active at the 1991 population census, 27,256 or 70.5 per cent were females. The majority among the non-economically active females were engaged in household work, while the majority among males were reported being in full-time education.

Women in public life

1. Although all males and females aged 21 years and over have been granted the voting right, women still remain marginalized in political decision-making processes, since only the

matai, who are mostly males, are eligible to contest various elections.

2. At present, there are two female *matai* among the 49 members of parliament. In 1994, only one of the 229 *pulenuu* or village council members was a woman.

3. Although about 53 per cent of all public sector employees in 1990 were females, women employees were largely concentrated at the lower levels of the service.

4. In 1994, there were five females functioning as executive heads of government departments; in that year a woman was also appointed for the first time to serve as a judge in the Lands and Titles Court. Currently, one of the four heads of diplomatic missions is a woman.

B. THE SETTING

1. Geography

The independent state of Samoa is located in the central South Pacific between 13° and 15° south latitude and 168° and 173° west longitude just to the east of the international date line. The country consists of two large islands (Savaii and Upolu), two small islands (Manono and Apolima) which lie between the two main islands, and five uninhabited islets lying off the coast of Upolu. The nearest neighbours are American Samoa, about 125 kilometres to the east; Tonga's northern islands, 200 kilometres to the south; and Fiji, over 600 kilometres to the south west.

The total land area of Samoa is 2,934 square kilometres or 1,100 square miles, which is the largest land area in Polynesia after French Polynesia. Unlike most other island countries of the region, the land area is not fragmented throughout a vast expanse of sea, but is almost entirely distributed between Savaii (1,820 square kilometres) and Upolu (1,100 square kilometres). Apia, the capital, is located in Upolu.

The larger islands have mountainous interiors of volcanic origin surrounded by fertile coastal plains. The interior mountain ranges rise

sharply to a maximum of 1,858 metres (6,095 feet) on the island of Savaii to 1,100 metres (3,605 feet) on Upolu. The islands volcanic origins have resulted in a terrain abundant with short and swift streams and waterfalls valuable for hydroelectric power. The greater part of the country is covered by lush vegetation and rain forest.

The climate is pleasantly tropical with wet and dry seasons. The average monthly temperature ranges from 20°C to 30°C with very limited seasonal variation. The rainy season extends from November through April and the average annual rainfall is about 287 centimetres. The Samoan islands lie outside the usual track of hurricanes but severe storms do occasionally strike. For example, Cyclone Val in December 1991 caused enormous damage to property and infrastructure in both the large islands.

2. Land use

Since the end of 1961, all lands have been legally classified as:

(a) Customary land held from the state in accordance with Samoan custom; that is, land traditionally vested in *matai* (chief) who holds the land in trust for their *aiga* (family group). Such land could be leased but not purchased. Customary land constitutes about 81 per cent of all land.

(b) Private freehold land which is held from the state in simple fee, constituting about four per cent of total land.

(c) Government land which is free from customary title and any estate in simple fee, constituting about 11 per cent of total land.

(d) Land under the control of Samoa Land Corporation (formerly Samoa Trust Estates Corporation), constituting four per cent of total land (table 1).

The customary land ownership, which was originally instituted to protect the rights of indigenous Samoans, has now become an indispensable part of the Samoan social system and of the rural economy. It has also proved to be an effective means of ensuring access to land

Table 1. Distribution of land by ownership

Ownership	Savaii		Upolu		Samoa	
	Square kilometres	Per cent	Square kilometres	Per cent	Square kilometres	Per cent
Customary land	1,532.7	88.8	767.9	69.0	2,300.6	81.0
Private free hold land	23.8	1.4	89.8	8.1	113.6	4.0
WESTEC	8.5	0.4	105.1	9.4	113.6.	4.0
Government land	161.8	9.4	150.4	13.5	312.2	11.0
Total	1,726.8	100.0	1,113.2	100.0	2,840.0	100.0

Source: Western Samoa's Sixth Development Plan, 1988-1990.

for subsistence purposes and thus providing food security to the community. Nevertheless, this traditional system is now increasingly recognized as a major constraint to diversification of land use and development of the economy. Land disputes between villages often result in valuable land remaining idle for extended periods. Besides, prolonged negotiations are usually required for government to obtain the necessary approvals for infrastructure or forestry development.

The cultivation of the customary land falls entirely under the direction of the *matai* who, as noted earlier, is the trustee of *aigas* customary lands. Female and male heirs have equal rights to *matai* titles, and while the daughters know their rights as an heir, cultivation and tilling of land is regarded as the responsibility of the sons; hence the daughters rarely claim land for themselves.

3. History and government

The first European settlers who came to the Samoan islands in the nineteenth century were missionaries, British and American traders, and German businessmen who established large coconut plantations that still exist to this day. European trade with Samoa increased and westerners became increasingly involved in internal affairs. Britain, Germany and the United States vied for control and after a brief period of joint responsibility, the islands were partitioned. The United States assumed control over the eastern islands (now American Samoa); Britain withdrew in lieu of claims elsewhere; and Germany assumed control over what is now Samoa.

At the outbreak of World War I, New Zealand occupied Samoa and administered the territories in various capacities, including those under a trusteeship of the United Nations. In 1962, Samoa became the first South Pacific country to gain independence from colonial rule.

Samoa has had *Fono* (a legislative assembly), which was composed of 47 members, of whom 45 were elected by *matai* suffrage; that is, by electors on a roll consisting entirely of *matai* (elected clan chiefs of small family units). In 1990, a plebiscite returned a result in favour of universal suffrage at age 21. The two other members in the assembly represent citizens of European extraction and are elected from a separate roll. In November 1991, the *Fono* approved legislation to increase the parliamentary term from three to five years and to create an additional two seats in the *Fono*.

In villages, local government still exists in its traditional form based on the *matai* system and the assembly in village *Fono*, which is the governing authority in each *nu'u* (parish). Most activities are organized around the villages, which tend to be politically, socially and economically self-sufficient.

Administrative districts based on geographical regions have been established and are primarily used by the central Government for operating health, education, police and agricultural services. Upolu is divided into three regions: Apia, the capital; North West Upolu; and the rest of Upolu. The island of Savaii is treated as one region. The smaller islands are included in the "rest of Upolu".

4. Population growth and distribution

a. Population growth

Samoa is the largest and the most populous among the Polynesian island nations. According to the latest census held in November 1991, the country's population was 161,298 with an increase of 124,955 from the 1921 census count of 36,343 persons. Although the population increased more than fourfold between 1921 and 1991, the rate of increase has not been uniform during this seventy-year period. The average annual rate of population growth has been fluctuating between 2.2 per cent and 3.7 per cent during the various intercensal periods up to 1951, but since 1956 the rate has declined steadily to a very low of 0.1 per cent during 1981-1986 and then rose to 0.5 per cent during 1986-1991 (table 2). Thus, the growth rates reflect a change from being one of the highest to one among the lowest in the world, especially within Asia-Pacific region.

The main factors responsible for the decline in the rate of population growth have been the fall in total fertility rate from 8.0 in 1962 to 4.7 in 1990 and the high level of emigration from Samoa particularly to New Zealand and American Samoa and, to a growing extent, to Australia and the United States of America (Hawaii and California). While being subjected

to annual fluctuations, the average annual net emigration was 4,450 during 1984-1991. It is estimated that at the end of the 1980s, approximately 100,000 to 130,000 or about 60 to 80 per cent of the country's population lived overseas. Although the number of emigrants has dwindled in recent years due to stringent immigration policies of principal recipient countries, the past large-scale emigration has reduced the rate of growth of the Samoan population.

In addition to depressing population growth rate, large-scale emigration from the country has also had extensive effects on the national economy and the way of life of the people. The substantial reduction in population growth has relieved the economy of the burdens or constraints normally associated with a burgeoning population. The remittances sent home by the emigrants also have contributed significantly to domestic individual incomes and the overall national income. Estimates indicate that remittances accounted for around 35 per cent of the nation's gross domestic product and that up to 40 to 50 per cent of disposable personal income may on average originate from remittances.

However, emigration on such a large scale has also had a number of detrimental effects on the country. Data from the censuses indicate that emigrants have, by and large, been

Table 2. Population of Samoa, intercensal increase, percentage increase and average annual growth rates: 1921 to 1991 censuses

Census year	Enumerated population	Intercensal increase	Percentage increase	Average annual growth rate (per cent)
1921	36,343	–	–	–
1926	40,229	3,886	10.7	2.2
1936	55,946	15,717	39.1	3.0
1945	68,197	12,251	21.9	2.2
1951	84,909	16,712	24.5	3.7
1956	97,327	12,418	14.6	2.7
1961	114,427	17,100	17.6	3.2
1966	131,377	16,950	14.8	2.8
1971	146,626	15,249	11.6	2.1
1976	151,983	5,357	3.7	0.7
1981	156,349	4,366	2.9	0.6
1986	157,158	809	0.5	0.1
1991	161,298	4,140	2.6	0.5

Source: South Pacific Commission, *Population Statistics*, Statistical Bulletin No. 42, 1995.

young people in the early stages of their economically active life with more than average educational and skill levels. The loss of young, ablebodied and educated persons has resulted in a shortage of labour and skill and contributed to high dependency ratios.

b. Population distribution

With the exception of the urban population of Apia, most of the Samoans live in about 360 villages largely located on the coastal plains of the two main islands of Savaii and Upolu. This compactness of population is unique in comparison with the Pacific neighbours of Samoa. Although Savaii is physically larger than Upolu, nearly three quarters (72.1 per cent) of the country's population lives on Upolu. Consequently, the average 1991 population density of Upolu (104 persons per square kilometre) is more than four times that of Savaii (table 3).

The main settlement area is the capital Apia and its environs; in 1991, Apia had the highest population density (565 persons per square kilometre), followed by North West Upolu (161 persons per square kilometre) and the rest of Upolu (54 persons per square kilometre). The concentration of modern development in Apia, such as employment and educational opportunities, attracts people from Savaii and the South and East of Upolu. Many of the coastal villages of North West Upolu have also gained people due to internal migration. The two cyclones which caused considerable damage to coastal areas, Ofa in 1990 and Val in 1991, have made people move to the interior

of the islands, and this movement is also facilitated by improved communication facilities.

5. Ethnicity and culture

The indigenous people of Samoa are Polynesians and they comprise the overwhelming majority (98 per cent) of the country's population. The remainder are part-Samoan who are mixed Europeans, Chinese, Fijians and Tongas, but this distinction is not of social importance. There are also some people living in Samoa from nearby closely related Polynesian groups, Tuvalu and Tokelau.

Samoan culture is similar to that of other Polynesian peoples; and the traditional Samoan way "faa Samoa", the central force, has remained strong despite long exposure to European influences. The *aiga*, or extended family, is the essential unit of the traditional social system. Each *aiga* is headed by a *matai*, a chief chosen by concensus of family members. As noted earlier, the *matai* has authority over land held in common by the *aiga* and is responsible for the welfare of the family members. The *matai* also serves on village councils which have wide powers.

Samoans have retained many traditional social practices which guides behaviour and maintain the Samoan way of life. Many aspects of collective communalism, in which family welfare takes precedence over individual rights, are still strong. Rituals and social conventions are fairly extensive and may appear complicated to an outsider.

Table 3. Numerical and percentage distribution of population by region, 1986 and 1991 and population density for 1991

Per cent	1986		1991		Population density (per square kilometre) 1991
	Number	Per cent	Number	Per cent	
Upolu	112,228	71.4	116,248	72.1	104
Apia Urban Area	32,196	20.5	34,126	21.2	565
North West Upolu	39,383	25.1	40,409	25.1	161
Rest of Upolu	40,649	25.9	41,713	25.9	54
Savaii	44,930	28.6	45,050	27.9	25
Samoa	157,158	100.0	161,298	100.0	55

Source: Department of Statistics, *Report of the Census of Population and Housing, 1991.*

The Samoan language is part of the vast Austronesian (Malayo-Polynesian) family of languages but has features which distinguish it from other nearby tongues. The language contains a large number of terms used when speaking to or even about persons of rank. Both Samoan and English are official languages; English is widely spoken and is the language used in conducting business in government departments and the commercial sector, whereas Samoan is used in the *Fono* (parliament) with simultaneous translation into English.

6. Religion

Samoans are very religious; religion plays a major role in traditional customs and social life of the people. The population is overwhelmingly Christian and Christianity is well integrated into the village social structure. Pastors have an important place in the village political hierarchy and church rituals and customs are taken seriously. Sundays are reserved almost excluvsively for church services.

The largest Christian denomination in Samoa is the Congregational Christian Church with 68,651 adherents or 42.5 per cent of the total population. Another about 21 per cent are Roman Catholics, while the rest of the Christians are Methodists, Later Day Saints and Seventh Day Adventists. Bahai and other small denominations account for 6 per cent of the population (table 4). Although the proportion of church membership between males and females is almost equal, women have very little say in the running of the church.

7. The economy

According to United Nations criteria, Samoa is one of the least developed countries in the world. The national economy is heavily dependent on agriculture and allied activities, including forestry and fishing. The agricultural sector, which accounts for one half of GDP and about 90 per cent of the export earnings, relies on a limited range of crops for domestic needs as well as exports, although attempts are being made to diversify the cash crops.

A substantial portion of the output originates in the traditional subsistence agriculture carried out within the extended family system and comprises 80 per cent of the area under cultivation and absorbs nearly two-thirds of the country's labour force. The most common subsistence crops are taros, yams, breadfruit and fruits. Several small plantations are engaged in commercial cropping. The major cash crops are coconuts and cocoa; copra historically was Samoa's main export. Taro, bananas, timber and coffee are also important cash crops.

Pigs, cattle, poultry and goats are raised mainly for local consumption. Development of livestock industry is hampered by animal diseases and shortage of skilled management. Fish and timber are the only exploitable large-scale natural resources. The seas surrounding Samoa have potentials for commercial fishing, but these resources are largely untapped.

The industrial sector contributes 10 per cent of GDP. Manufacturing is principally con-

Table 4. Numerical and percentage distribution of population by religion and sex: 1991

Religion	Both sexes		Male		Female	
	Number	Per cent	Number	Per cent	Number	Per cent
Congregationalist	68,651	42.6	36,061	42.6	32,590	42.5
Catholic	33,548	20.8	17,426	20.6	16,122	21.0
Methodist	27,190	16.9	14,360	17.0	12,830	16.7
Later day saints	16,394	10.2	8,539	10.1	7,855	10.2
Seventh day adventist	4,685	2.9	2,428	2.9	2,257	2.9
Other regions	9,460	5.9	4,992	5.9	4,468	5.8
Not stated	1,370	0.8	795	0.9	575	0.7
Total	161,298	100.0	84,601	100.0	76,697	100.0

Source: Department of Statistics, *Report of the Census of Population and Housing, 1991.*

cerned with small-scale production of coconut-based products, food, garments, construction materials, leather goods, cigarettes and beer. Most of the industrial enterprises are located near Apia, the capital. Tourism has been an important foreign exchange earner and provides much direct and indirect employment.

In recent years, economic development has been adversely affected by inclement weather, limited agricultural exports and inadequate transport facilities. Samoa is vulnerable to fluctuations in the price of copra and cocoa on the international market. Since late 1993, output of taro, the country's staple food, was affected by the taro leaf blight, which hit the plantations throughout the islands. The widespread damage to crops, buildings and the islands' infrastructure caused by the cyclones in 1990 and 1991 had imposed a heavy burden on the country's financial resources.

8. Social infrastructure

Samoa's social indicators are generally favourable as compared with most Pacific developing countries. Substantial progress has been made in increasing enrolments at the primary and secondary levels of education, while adult literacy of 98 per cent is among the highest in the world. Overall health has improved in recent years; infant mortality is comparatively low and life expectancy at birth has increased over the years. A high proportion of households has been provided with access to safe water and sanitation.

a. Education

Education is administered by the Department of Education and has been compulsory for all children under age 14 years since 1992. The Samoan education system, which is based on the New Zealand system, comprises three levels: primary education accommodating children aged 5-12 years up to standard IV; intermediate level attended for two or three years by students between ages 12 and 15; and secondary education, which students usually enter at the age of 15, may account for another four or five years, although students may choose to leave at the end of the second or fourth year according to their ability.

In 1991, there were 141 primary schools under the Ministry of Education, of which 140 were owned by the villages but staffed by government teachers. Only the Apia Primary School is fully owned and staffed by the government. In 1989, there were 21 junior secondary schools staffed by government teachers and managed by the districts. In addition to government schools, there are also 18 primary and 21 junior secondary schools operated by religious organizations which work in cooperation with the Education Department.

Although education is not free, the value placed on it is reflected in the high proportion of children attending schools. Over the last two decades, there has been significant increase in the proportion of children attending school; estimates indicate that the proportion of children aged 5-19 years at school increased from 72.1 per cent in 1971 to approximately 85.0 per cent in 1986.

Tertiary education in Samoa is available through the National University of Samoa; admissions are restricted to those who have completed grade 13 and sat for an entrance examination. There is also a trades training institute, a teacher training college and a college for tropical agriculture (the second campus of University of South Pacific located in Alafua near Apia).

b. Health

Most health services are in the public sector and are administered under the authority of the Health Department. Health care is provided through a hierarchical system which includes one national hospital in Apia; 13 district hospitals, of which 7 are in rural Upolu and 6 in Savaii; and 20 health sub-centres. The national hospital with 290 beds provides services for the residents of the capital and takes referrals from the rest of the country. A network of radio telephones connects the district hospitals and the health sub-centres in remote areas to the national hospital. Each village also has a women's committee to promote health activities in the local community. All public health facilities in Samoa charge fees and have done so over the past ten years or so.

Public health services include those devoted to maternal and child health, family planning, immunization programmes, support services for persons suffering from tuberculosis and leprosy, as well as sanitary inspections. An extensive school health programme includes routine checks for skin problems, oral health, immunization and dressing for wounds and sores.

Overall health status in terms of morbidity and mortality has improved over the past two decades. Many infectious diseases such as measles, polio, leprosy and tuberculosis are largely under control as a consequence of past investments in public health programmes. There has also been a decline in the number of reported cases of sexually transmitted diseases. The progress achieved is reflected in relevant health indicators. For instance, infant mortality rate has declined dramatically from 63 in 1970 to 22 in 1991; life expectancy at birth has increased over the years and in 1990 was estimated at 64 years for males and 67 years for females.

Nevertheless, Samoa is currently facing a range of health problems. The changing life styles of the Samoan people towards less physical activity and high levels of consumption of sugar, fat, tobacco and alcohol have led to growing importance of non-communicable "life style" diseases, as reflected in an increase in dental caries, hypertension, diabetes and obesity (see annex table B.1). Further, the crowded urban living conditions and poor water and sanitation are considered to be the cause of rising incidence of gastro-intestinal diseases.

As a consequence of the large-scale emigration of trained personnel, health authorities are faced with overriding human resources issues. The public health system suffers a shortage of doctors and nurses with many doctors over the age of retirement and many others on aid or volunteer projects. In 1992, there was one doctor per 2,701 persons and one nurse per 544 persons. In the rural areas, where about 70 per cent of the population live, there were only 7 doctors, while 45 doctors worked at the national hospital in urban Apia.

c. *Housing and sanitation*

In the rural areas, housing is still a community activity and housing structures have largely conformed to traditional designs or styles known as *"fales"*, using locally available materials. *Fales* consists of a thatched roof supported by posts with no permanent walls. The sides have pandanas mats that can be rolled down in the evening or during rainy weather. However, on account of the frequency of cyclones in recent years, there is an increasing tendency to rebuild the houses using modern imported materials. Corrugated galvanized iron is used in place of thatch for roof and concrete is poured for the foundation. Others have permanent walls in place.

Samoa has a comparatively high coverage in regard to piped wear, but there are problems related to the quality of services. While coverage is nearly 100 per cent in Apia urban area, in the rural areas untreated reticulated water systems cover about 60 per cent of the communities on Savaii and 85 per cent on Upolu islands. The country experiences periodic shortages of water due to lack of surface water resources, insufficient storage capacity and seasonal factors. Water quality is also inadequate; contaminated water is the source of gastro-intestinal infections causing diarrhoea. The proportion of the population relying on rain water is twice as high in Savaii as in the other three regions.

The use of sanitary facilities for disposal of human excreta is almost universal in the Apia urban area, where houses have been provided with septic toilets, water sealed latrines or pit toilets. In the rural areas, 60 per cent of the households used sealed latrines, while a further 20 per cent used properly constructed pit toilets in 1991 (table 5).

In the urban areas, 93 per cent of the living quarters use electricity for lighting, compared with 75 per cent in all rural areas and 74 per cent in Savaii. The majority of the remaining living quarters use benzine or kerosine for lighting. Although electricity is available in most areas, only 15 per cent of urban households and 5 per cent of rural households

Table 5. Percentage of living quarters with different toilet facilities by region: 1991

Toilet facilities	Total	Apia urban area	North West of Upolu	Rest of Upolu	Savaii
Flush with septic tank	44	68	47	36	30
Pisikoa type	46	29	39	54	57
Pit without septic tank	9	3	12	8	11
Other	1	0	2	2	2
Total	100	100	100	100	100

Source: Department of Statistics, *Report of the Census of Population and Housing, 1991.*

Note: Pisikoa type = pour-flush toilets introduced by the Peace Corps.

use electricity for cooking purposes. Firewood still remains the most common fuel for cooking with 55 per cent of urban and 76 per cent of rural living quarters using firewood.

Eighty-four per cent of all households in the country own a radio; the proportion in the urban areas (87 per cent) is slightly higher than that in the rural areas (83 per cent).

C. WOMEN'S PROFILE

1. Demographic characteristics

a. Sex composition

In Samoa, males outnumber females in the total population. This excess of males over females is not an accident of any one census, but has been an important demographic feature highlighted by all 13 census enumerations since 1921. According to these censuses, the propor-

tionate share of females in the country's population has varied from 47 to 49 per cent. At the last census held in 1991, females constituted 47.5 per cent of the total population; in other words, there were about 91 females for every 100 males or 110 males per 100 females in the country.

The excess of males over females appears to have been the result of a combination of factors, such as a male-favoured sex ratio at birth and underenumeration of females at the censuses. Evidence from many countries from various parts of the globe clearly indicates that the number of male births generally exceeds the number of females every year and Samoa is no exception to this biological phenomenon. Although accurate information is not available, it is generally believed that in the past females experienced a mortality rate that was higher than that of males. It is also suspected that as in most developing countries, females

Table 6. Population classified by sex, percentage of female and sex ratio: 1921 to 1991

Census year	Enumerated population			Per cent female	Sex ratio	
	Both sexes	Male	Female		Male per 100 female	Female per 100 male
1921	36,343	19,442	16,901	46.5	115.0	86.9
1926	40,229	20,981	19,248	47.8	109.0	91.7
1936	55,946	28,727	27,219	48.7	105.5	94.8
1945	68,197	35,107	33,090	48.5	106.1	94.3
1951	84,909	43,790	41,119	48.4	106.4	93.9
1956	97,327	49,863	47,464	48.8	105.1	95.2
1961	114,427	58,785	55,642	48.6	105.6	94.7
1966	131,377	67,842	63,535	48.4	106.8	93.7
1971	146,627	75,950	70,677	48.2	107.4	93.1
1976	151,983	78,639	73,344	48.3	107.2	93.3
1981	156,349	81,027	75,322	48.2	107.6	93.0
1986	157,158	83,247	73,911	47.0	112.6	88.8
1991	161,298	84,601	76,697	47.5	110.3	90.7

Source: South Pacific Commission, *Population Statistics,* Statistical Bulletin No. 42, 1995.

tend to be underreported in the various enumerations and investigations.

The overall sex ratios, however, conceal the variations in these measures between urban and rural areas as well as across various age groups. It will be noted from table 7 that while males outnumber females in both the urban and rural areas, there are relatively more women in the urban than in the rural areas. For instance, in 1991 females constituted 48.2 per cent of the urban population but 47.4 per cent of the rural population. Similar disparities are also noticeable in all census years. This pattern appears to be unique to Samoa, because in most other countries there are relatively more females in the rural areas on account of the

preponderance of males in the rural-to-urban migration streams.

The numerical distributions of the enumerated population by five-year age groups and sex for four censuses from 1976 to 1991 are given in annex table C.1. The age-specific sex ratios derived from these distributions are given in table 8.

It is clear from table 8 that in all four census counts males have outnumbered females at the young age groups, 0-24 years, while there was an excess of females over males at the migration-prone ages, 25-49 years, in 1976, at ages 30-49 in 1981, and at ages 35-44 in 1986. But in 1991, females were

Table 7. Enumerated population classified by urban and rural area and sex, percentage of female and sex ratios: 1971 to 1991

Census year	Urban area					Rural areas				
	Male	Female	Per cent female	Male per 100 female	Female per 100 male	Male	Female	Per cent female	Male per 100 female	Female per 100 male
1971	15,404	14,857	49.1	103.7	96.4	60,546	55,820	48.0	108.4	92.2
1976	16,400	15,699	48.9	104.4	95.7	62,239	57,645	48.1	108.0	92.6
1981	16,953	16,217	48.9	104.5	95.7	64,074	59,105	48.0	108.4	92.2
1986	16,853	15,343	47.7	109.8	91.0	66,394	58,568	46.9	113.4	88.2
1991	17,686	16,440	48.2	107.6	93.0	66,915	60,257	47.4	111.0	90.1

Source: Department of Statistics.

Table 8. Age-specific sex ratios: 1976, 1981, 1986 and 1991 censuses

Age group	Male per 100 female				Female per 100 male			
	1976	1981	1986	1991	1976	1981	1986	1991
0-4	111.5	112.3	116.5	108.1	89.7	89.1	85.8	92.4
5-9	110.8	110.4	115.6	111.6	90.5	90.5	86.4	89.6
10-14	107.1	112.2	117.6	111.2	93.3	89.1	85.1	89.9
15-19	113.6	109.4	118.9	118.5	88.0	91.4	84.1	84.4
20-24	115.4	110.3	116.5	125.4	86.6	90.6	85.8	79.7
25-29	97.6	105.6	109.4	113.8	102.4	94.7	91.4	87.9
30-34	97.1	98.9	103.6	108.0	102.9	101.1	96.5	92.6
35-39	99.0	97.4	99.3	102.8	101.0	102.6	100.7	97.3
40-44	99.3	99.1	99.2	100.7	100.7	100.9	100.8	99.3
45-49	99.7	98.8	101.8	99.7	100.3	101.2	98.2	100.3
50-54	102.6	102.4	105.4	99.8	97.4	97.7	94.9	100.2
55-59	106.4	111.7	111.3	105.2	94.0	89.5	89.8	95.1
60-64	105.5	102.7	113.8	100.4	94.8	97.4	87.9	99.5
65-69	103.2	101.3	118.0	106.0	96.9	98.7	84.8	94.3
70-74	99.7	95.0	104.8	93.1	100.3	105.3	95.4	107.4
75+	73.4	72.1	89.0	78.6	136.1	138.6	112.4	127.3
All ages	107.2	107.6	112.6	110.3	93.3	93.0	88.8	90.7

Source: Department of Statistics.

14

more than males at ages 45-54 years. At the older ages, 70 years and over, women outnumber men due to the relatively higher female life expectancy at these ages.

It may also be noted that between 1986 and 1991 the number of males per 100 females at ages 0-19 has declined due perhaps to a fall in female mortality at these ages, while the ratio of males per 100 females at ages 20-44 has increased due perhaps to greater propensity among females in these ages to emigrate. It is also significant to note that the sex ratio for the 0-4 age group, which is largely determined by the sex ratio at birth, appears to be rather high, suggesting a higher sex ratio at birth than the world average and higher mortality among female infants and children.

b. Age structure

The age structure of the population is determined by past trends in the levels of fertility, mortality and international migration. The percentage distribution of the Samoan population as enumerated at the four censuses from 1976 to 1991 is given in annex table C.2. It will be noted from this table that in 1991 the percentage share of the total population was highest at the youngest age group, 0-4 years, for both males and females, reflecting largely the number of births, and deaths among these births, that have occurred during the five years preceding the 1991 census. It will also be noted that the age-specific proportions decreasing with advancing ages reflect the effect of mortality and migration (also see figure 1). However, the very sharp decrease in the proportions roughly be-

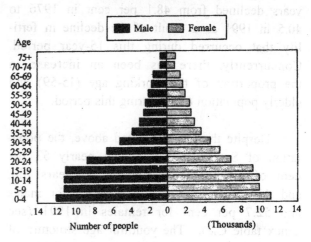

Figure 1. Age structure of the Samoan population: 1991

Source: Department of Statistics.

tween ages 20 and 49 has to be attributed more to overseas migration, because the bulk of these migrants belong to the prime working ages, than to the effects of the mortality at these ages, which normally is very low.

Like in most developing countries, a very high proportion of Samoan population is below the age of 15 years. In 1991, children aged 0-14 years constituted about 41 per cent of the total population, this proportion was the same for males and females. People in the working ages accounted for around 53 per cent of the population (53.8 per cent for males and 53.0 per cent for females). Elderly persons aged 60 years and over constituted about 6 per cent of the population; the proportion of elderly women (6.4 per cent) was slightly higher than the corresponding male proportion (5.6 per cent), reflecting the higher mortality among men at these ages (see table 9).

Table 9. Percentage distribution of enumerated population and dependency ratio by broad age group and sex: 1976, 1981, 1986 and 1991 censuses

Age group	1976			1981			1986			1991		
	Both sexes	Male	Female	Both sexes	Male	Female	Both sexes	Male	Female	Both sexes	Male	Female
0-14	48.1	48.7	47.7	44.2	45.1	43.4	41.2	41.9	40.5	40.5	40.6	40.6
15-59	47.4	46.9	47.4	51.0	49.6	51.5	53.2	52.6	53.9	53.4	53.8	53.0
60+	4.5	4.4	4.9	4.8	4.5	5.1	5.6	5.5	5.6	6.1	5.6	6.4
Total	100.0	100.0	100.0	100.0	100.0	100.0	100.0	100.0	100.0	100.0	100.0	100.0
Dependency ratio	111.6	113.0	110.1	98.9	100.9	96.8	87.9	89.8	85.7	87.4	86.1	89.0

Source: Department of Statistics.

It will also be observed from table 9 that the proportionate share of children aged 0-14 years declined from 48.1 per cent in 1976 to 40.5 in 1991 as a result of the decline in fertility that occurred during this 15-year period. Concurrently, there has been an increase in the proportion of the working age (15-59) and elderly population (65+) during this period.

Despite the changes noted above, the population of Samoa is still young, nearly 53 per cent of all people are below 20 years old, and this proportion is 53.6 per cent for males and 52.7 per cent for females in 1991 (see annex table C.2). The youthful age structure of the population has both economic and demographic implications. A concentration of the population at the very young and dependent ages means that the number of persons at the working age is disproportionately small in relation to the unprotective groups, who are dependent on them. Thus, in Samoa, every 100 persons aged 15-59 year have to support about 87 persons in the dependent age group, 0-14 and 60 and over. Demographically, the current youthful age structure has built-in momentum for further rapid increase of the population over the next few decades.

c. Marital status

According to the 1991 census data, half the males and a little over a third of the females aged 15 years and over were reported single or unmarried. The census also revealed that the proportion reported married, widowed and separated/divorced was higher among females, compared with males (table 10). The higher proportion of single men is due to the fact that men marry at an older age than women. The higher incidence of widowhood among women is largely due to their higher life expectancy vis-a-vis men and the greater prospects of remarriage for widowers, compared with widows. The latter reason also explains the higher rate of divorce/separation among women.

It is also clear from table 10 that between 1986 and 1991, there has been an increase in the proportion of single men and a decrease in this proportion among women. There has also been a substantial increase in the proportion

Table 10. Percentage distribution of population aged 15 years and over by marital status and sex: 1986 and 1991

Marital status	1986		1991	
	Male	Female	Male	Female
Single	49	38	50	36
Married	48	54	47	54
Widowed, divorced/ separated	3	8	3	10
All statuses	100	100	100	100

Source: Department of Statistics, *Report of the Census of Population and Housing, 1991.*

of widowed, separated and divorced among women between 1986 and 1991.

d. International migration

As noted in the previous section, international migration plays an important role in Samoa's population growth. Despite high rates of natural increase, overall population growth rates remain very low because of substantial emigration of Samoans overseas, particularly to American Samoa. In recent years, women have constituted an increasing proportion of those leaving the country; in 1990-1992, women constituted about 45 per cent of all emigrants from Samoa (see table 11).

The somewhat incomplete data for 1990-1992 period also suggests that 76 per cent of males and 78 per cent of females emigrated for "other" reasons. While the proportion of those emigrating for educational purposes was almost the same for males and females, a higher proportion among males (20.8 per cent), compared with females (15.7 per cent), emigrated for employment reasons.

2. Educational background

Data from the Education Department show that there has been a steady increase in educational enrolment rates for both boys and girls between 1971 and 1986 and that enrolment rates of girls have been higher than the corresponding rates of boys at all age groups between 5 and 19 years. In 1986, nearly 86 per cent of all girls and 77 per cent of all boys aged 5-19 years attended school, and in that year

Table 11. Numerical and percentage distribution of departees by purpose and sex: 1990-1992

Purpose	Both sexes		Male		Female	
	Number	Per cent	Number	Per cent	Number	Per cent
Employment	16,178	18.5	10,079	20.8	6,099	15.7
Education	2,703	3.1	1,535	3.2	1,168	3.0
Other	68,458	78.4	36,772	76.0	31,686	81.3
Total	87,339	100.0	48,386	100.0	38,953	100.0

Source: Western Samoa, *Migration Dataset, 1990-1992.*

Note: Information relating to the last six months of 1990, October 1991, and July and August 1992 were missing and not available at the time of preparing this report.

Samoa was within striking distance of attaining universal primary education; 88.4 per cent of children aged 5-9 years and 81.3 per cent of children in the age group of 10-14 years were reported enrolled in the schools (table 12 and annex table C.3).

The trends and differentials in school enrolment rates reflected in the data from the Education Department are also confirmed by the population census data on school participation, although the rates based on census figures are somewhat lower than those based on Education Department statistics. According to the 1991 population census, 88 per cent of females and 84 per cent of males aged 5-19 years were reported being in full-time education. The universality of primary and early secondary education is also apparent from the responses of persons aged 10-14 years; nearly 98 per cent of girls and 97 per cent of boys in this age group were claimed to be full-time students. At ages 15-19, approximately 75 per cent of the girls and 66 per cent of the boys were in full-time education (table 13).

It is also clear from table 13 that there have been improvements in school participation rates between 1981 and 1991 and that these improvements were quite marked at all ages, 5-19 years. According to both censuses, participation rates of girls were significantly higher

Table 12. School enrolment rates by age group and sex: 1971, 1976, 1981 and 1986 censuses

Age group	1971			1976			1981			1986		
	Both sexes	Male	Female	Both sexes	Male	Female	Both sexes	Male	Female	Both sexes	Male	Female
5-9	73.6	73.0	74.2	82.0	82.1	81.8	81.1	80.6	81.6	88.4	86.8	90.1
10-14	92.4	90.3	94.7	93.0	93.0	96.1	97.5	96.6	98.4	81.3	76.3	87.1
15-19	43.8	41.1	46.9	49.6	49.6	58.7	64.9	60.6	69.7	74.4	68.6	81.2
5-19	72.1	70.4	74.1	76.4	76.4	80.3	81.8	80.1	83.7	81.3	77.2	86.2

Source: Department of Education.

Table 13. Educational participation rates by age group and sex: 1981 and 1991 censuses

(percentage)

Age group	1981 census			1991 census		
	Both sexes	Male	Female	Both sexes	Male	Female
5-9	81	81	82	89	88	89
10-14	97	97	98	98	97	98
15-19	65	61	70	70	66	75
5-19	82	80	84	86	84	88

Source: Department of Statistics, *Report of the Census of Population and Housing, 1991.*

than the corresponding rates of boys at ages 15-19 years.

According to the 1991 census, 97.8 per cent of females and 98.6 per cent of males aged 15 years and over were literate.

D. WOMEN IN FAMILY LIFE

1. The Samoan family

In Samoa, as in many other societies, family is the most important social organization, providing its members with basic needs such as food, clothing and shelter. It is also the main determinant of the survival of children and the only institutional support structure for the elderly persons. Family members share a unique social and cultural environment that defines roles and obligations, shapes values and beliefs, provides enjoyment and exerts influence. Family welfare takes precedence over individual rights and individuals are obligated to assist a family member, whenever assistance was requested.

Irrespective of actual living arrangements, the term "family" in Samoa usually means "extended family", which, as noted earlier, is the core element of the traditional culture. The head of the family is the *matai* who is usually a male, although the work and contribution of women to the development and maintenance of the family are indispensable. Although the system has inherent rigidity, certain practices contribute to its flexibility. For example, respect for age is tempered by a recognition of the ability of younger and better educated members who support the family. This has resulted in an increase in the number of young and well-educated *matais*.

As a result of urbanization and migration, the extended family system is being gradually replaced by the nuclear family structure. Nuclear families are more evident in Apia urban area, while the extended family is still the chief social organization in the rural areas.

2. Family formation

According to the data on marital status gathered at the 1991 census, nearly 59 per cent

of females and 85 per cent of males in the age group of 20-24 years have remained single or never-married. Even at the next higher age group, 25-29 years, a quarter of the females and more than half of the males were reported single (table 14).

Table 14. Age-specific proportions of never-married and currently married persons aged 15 years and over by sex: 1991 census

Age group	Never married		Currently married	
	Male	Female	Male	Female
15-19	98.9	94.1	1.0	5.3
20-24	85.4	59.4	13.9	36.9
25-29	52.8	25.8	45.7	68.8
30-34	26.3	14.3	71.5	79.7
35-39	16.9	8.4	81.0	84.6
40-44	13.0	6.8	83.6	84.9
45-49	8.6	5.6	87.7	84.9
50-54	7.8	5.2	88.4	80.7
55-59	8.5	5.8	86.3	74.8
60+	7.4	6.6	80.3	51.3
All ages 15+	50.0	35.7	47.2	54.5

Source: Department of Statistics, *Report of the Census of Population and Housing, 1991.*

The relatively high proportions of those remaining unmarried at generally popular marriage ages would suggest that there is a strong tendency among young persons to refrain from early marriage but enter into marital union at a later stage (also see figure 2). This tendency is also confirmed by the fact that the proportions of those remaining single decreases and those currently married increases with advan-

Figure 2. Certified marriages by age of bride and groom: 1988 to 1993

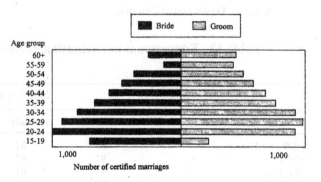

Source: Department of Statistics.

Note: At age 60+, 17 bride and 18 groom with age not stated are included.

18

cing ages. Among females, nearly 80 per cent or more were reported currently married at ages 30-54 years, while more than 80 per cent of all males were currently married at ages 35 and over. Only around 5 per cent of females and 8 per cent of males remained single at ages 50 and over.

It is also evident from table 14 that the proportion of never-married persons was significantly higher among males than among females at all age groups and that this gender differential was more marked at ages 20-44 years. The higher proportion of single males could largely be attributed to their older age at marriage; the 1991 singulate mean age at marriage was 28.3 years for males and 24.3 years for females. This would mean that, by and large, men marry women who are at least four years younger than them.

3. Reproductive behaviour

According to estimates based on the 1991 census data, the total fertility rate, or the total number of children that would have been born to a woman during her lifetime if she were to pass through her children-bearing ages conforming to the age-specific fertility rates of a given period, was 4.76. The 1991 age-specific fertility rates show that these rates peaked at ages 25-34 years and declined sharply at older ages, especially beyond 40 years of age (table 15).

Although the total fertility rate is estimated to have declined from 6.7 in 1981 to 4.8 in 1991, the current fertility rate is considered high in comparison with other Polynesian island countries such as French Polynesia, the Cook Islands, Niue, and Wallis and Futuna. The high

Table 15. Age-specific fertility rates: 1991

Age group	Age-specific fertility rate
15-19	0.025
20-24	0.159
25-29	0.241
30-34	0.216
35-39	0.175
40-44	0.098
45-49	0.038
Total fertility rate	4.76

Source: Department of Statistics, *Report of the Census of Population and Housing, 1991.*

fertility is largely due to the fact that family planning services cover only about 28 per cent of women at child-bearing ages.

According to data published by the Department of Health, nearly two thirds of those who accepted family planning used Depo Provera (43.0 per cent) and oral pills (23.5 per cent) in 1992 (table 16). Recent studies indicate that the drop-outs from family planning methods are increasing, mainly due to a desire for pregnancy and the inability of the services to maintain contact with the users.

Table 16. Numerical and percentage distribution of contraceptive users by method: 1991 and 1992

Contraceptive method	1991		1992	
	Number	Per cent	Number	Per cent
Depo Provera	2,849	45.6	2,393	43.0
Oral pills	1,689	27.1	1,307	23.5
Intrauterine device	660	10.6	730	13.1
Tubal ligation	565	9.1	565	10.1
Condom	479	7.7	540	9.7
Other[a]	1	0.0	33	0.6
All methods	6,243	100.0	5,568	100.0

[a] Refers to the use of calendar rhythm etc.

Source: Department of Health, *Annual Report, 1991 and 1992.*

It will also be noted from table 16 that the total number of contraceptors has declined from 6,243 in 1991 to 5,568 in 1992. In Samoa, although women have the choice to have children and the freedom to determine the number of children they wish to have, their spouse as well as the elderly in-laws exercise a great influence on their reproductive life.

4. Maternal and child health

The relatively high fertility rates place a considerable health burden on women and children. However, the maternal and child health services have been successful in reaching the majority of pregnant women. These services are operated through the Family Welfare Centre in Apia and through the district nurses in the rural areas. These district nurses deliver all services related to maternal and child health as well as family planning.

According to the data of the Health Department, about 55 per cent of pregnant women attended antenatal clinics in 1992 with an average of three visits per woman. A 1994 World Bank study observed that despite easy access to health facilities throughout the country, a substantial number of deliveries take place at home and that, although reliable data are not available, the extent of delivery complications is considered significant. According to the Health Department, about three quarters of all births in 1991-1992 were attended by qualified health personnel and there has been a decline in the number of births delivered by traditional birth attendants between 1988 and 1992 (see annex table D.1).

Maternal mortality during the period 1988-1990 has been estimated at 50 per 100,000 live births. Given an average of 4.8 births per woman during her reproductive span, there is a 1 in 426 chance of a woman dying as a result of complications during pregnancy and child birth.

The Expanded Programme of Immunization, which was launched in 1980, has attained a very high coverage. According to the Health Department, in 1992 about 98 per cent of infants received BCG immunization against tuberculosis; 92 per cent received the three doses necessary for full immunization against diphtheria, pertussis and tetanus; 92 per cent received the complete doses against polio; and 94 per cent were immunized against measles.

For children below five years, malnutrition and being underweight have become a major health problem due largely to underfeeding, inadequate protein intake, low incomes and large family size. The problem is considered more severe in urban than in rural areas.

According to recent United Nations estimates, infant mortality rate in Samoa has declined from 158 per 1,000 births in 1950-1955 to 64 per 1,000 births in 1990-1995. However, estimates based on the Health Department data give an infant mortality rate of 25 per 1,000 live births in 1992.

Estimates prepared by the United Nations also indicate that life expectancy at birth has been consistently higher for females than for males. During the past four decades, female life expectancy increased from 45.0 years to 69.2 years, while male life expectancy increased from 43.0 years to 65.9 years (table 17).

Table 17. Life expectancy at birth by sex: 1950-1955 to 1990-1995

(years)

Period	Life expectancy at birth		
	Both sexes	Male	Female
1950-1955	44.0	43.0	45.0
1955-1960	48.2	47.0	49.5
1960-1965	51.4	50.0	53.0
1965-1970	55.1	53.0	57.5
1970-1975	58.5	57.0	60.0
1975-1980	61.5	60.0	63.0
1980-1985	63.5	62.0	65.0
1985-1990	65.5	64.0	67.0
1990-1995	67.6	65.9	69.2

Source: United Nations, *World Population Prospects: The 1994 Revision.*

5. Marital disruption

Persons who are divorced/separated or widowed constitute the segment of the population living in a state of marital disruption. According to the 1991 census data, a higher proportion of females (9.8 per cent) than of males (2.7 per cent) aged 15 years and over were reported either divorced/separated or widowed (table 18).

Table 18. Age-specific proportions of divorced/separated and widowed persons aged 15 years and over by sex: 1991 census

(percentage)

Age group	Divorced/separated		Widowed	
	Male	Female	Male	Female
15-19	–	0.4	0.1	0.2
20-24	0.5	3.1	0.2	0.6
25-29	1.2	4.6	0.3	0.8
30-34	1.8	4.8	0.4	1.2
35-39	1.7	4.7	0.4	2.3
40-44	2.5	3.8	0.8	4.5
45-49	2.4	3.6	1.3	5.9
50-54	2.3	3.9	1.5	10.2
55-59	2.3	3.3	2.9	16.1
60+	2.6	2.9	9.7	39.2
All ages	1.3	3.1	1.4	6.7

Source: Department of Statistics, *Report of the Census of Population and Housing, 1991.*

It will be noted from table 18 that the incidence of divorce/separation as well as widowhood was higher for females than for males at all age groups. The proportion of widowed persons at older ages among females was markedly higher than among males; at ages 60 and over, nearly 39 per cent of females and about 10 per cent of males were reported widowed. The higher incidence of widowhood among females could be attributed to two factors: higher life expectancy of females than that of males, and the greater likelihood of a widowed male to remarry, compared with his female counterpart. The latter reason would also largely explains the higher rate of divorce/separation among females than among males.

6. Family/household structure

The 1991 Census enumerated a total of 21,928 households in Samoa. With a total enumerated population of 161,298, the average household size amounted to 7.4 persons.

According to the 1992 Women in Agriculture Survey, an extended family in Samoa consisted of an average 13.3 members: 3.7 adult males, 3.8 adult females and 5.8 children below 15 years of age. The average size and composition of the extended family/household, however, varied between Upolu and Savaii. In Upolu, an average extended family consisted of 11.2 members, compared with 14.6 in Savaii, and the average number of adult females was significantly higher in Savaii than in Upolu (table 19).

According to the 1991 Population and Housing Census, only 3,621 or 16.5 per cent

Table 19. Average size and composition of extended family/household by region: 1992

Region	Average household size			
	Total	Adult male	Adult female	Children below 15
Samoa	13.3	3.7	3.8	5.8
Upolu	11.2	3.6	3.1	4.5
Savaii	14.6	3.7	4.3	6.6

Source: Department of Agriculture and Ministry of Women's Affairs, *Report on Women in Agriculture Survey: Summary, 1993.*

of the 21,928 households in the country were headed by women. The census also revealed that while 88.6 per cent of male heads were married, 53.7 per cent of female household heads were widowed, another 10.8 per cent were single, and a further 8.8 per cent were separated/divorced (table 20). Thus, in Samoa, as in many other countries, women generally assume headship roles only in the absence of a male head.

Table 20. Numerical and percentage distribution of household heads by marital status and sex: 1991

Marital status	Male heads		Female heads	
	Number	Per cent	Number	Per cent
Single	1,286	7.0	392	10.8
Married	16,212	88.6	967	26.7
Separated/ divorced	288	1.6	318	8.8
Windowed	521	2.8	1,944	53.7
Total	18,307	100.0	3,621	100.0

Source: Department of Statistics, *Report of the Census of Population and Housing, 1991.*

7. Domestic violence

Reliable and comprehensive information and data on domestic violence are not available, since most cases of domestic violence, whether against males or females, are for various reasons not reported to the authorities. However, an idea of the stress undergone by men and women could be obtained from the records on suicide attempts and resultant deaths maintained by the Apia National Hospital for the period 1988-1992 (table 21).

It will be noted from table 21 that there was a total of 184 cases of attempted suicide of which 117 or 63.6 per cent were by men and 67 or 36.4 per cent were by women. It is also evident from the table that 101 of the 184 attempted suicide cases or 54.9 per cent have resulted in deaths; this proportion was 52.2 per cent for females and 56.4 per cent for males. It will also be noted that 88.0 per cent of the cases of attempted suicide among males and 86.6 per cent of the cases among females related to persons aged 11 to 35 years. The largest number of cases of attempted suicide

Table 21. Numerical and percentage distribution of the cases admitted to Apia National Hospital of suicide attempts and resultant deaths by age group and sex: 1988-1992

Age group	Both sexes				Male				Female			
	Attempt		Death		Attempt		Death		Attempt		Death	
	Num-ber	Per cent	Num-ber	Per cent	Num-ber	Per cent	Num-ber	Per cent	Num-ber	Per cent	Num-ber	Per cent
11-15	11	6.0	2	2.0	8	6.8	1	1.5	3	4.5	1	2.9
16-20	56	30.4	39	38.6	28	23.9	20	30.3	28	41.8	19	54.3
21-25	47	25.5	24	23.8	30	25.6	16	24.2	17	25.4	8	22.9
26-30	36	19.6	15	14.9	29	24.8	12	18.2	7	10.4	3	8.6
31-35	11	6.0	5	5.0	8	6.8	3	4.5	3	4.5	2	5.7
35+	23	12.5	16	15.8	14	12.0	14	21.2	9	13.4	2	5.7
Total	184	100.0	101	100.0	117	100.0	66	100.0	67	100.0	35	100.0

Source: Department of Health.

was in the age group 16-20 years for females and at ages 21-25 for males.

E. WOMEN IN ECONOMIC LIFE

1. Database

In Samoa, as in most Pacific island countries, women play a very important role in economic production, particularly in subsistence agriculture and household economic activities. However, as is common in subsistence oriented economies, their participation in economic activity and contribution to economic production have not been fully acknowledged in official statistics. Since women largely combine their economic activities with household duties, there has been a tendency in the past census enumerations to classify them as housewives. The problem may have been further compounded by the fact that in responding to the relevant census questions, women themselves may not have considered their part-time involvement in subsistence production as constituting economic activity.

The underreporting of female economic activity is reflected in their very low economic activity rates vis-a-vis the male rates at the three censuses from 1976 to 1986. According to these censuses, while the economic activity rates for males aged 15 years and over were more than 75 per cent, the corresponding female rates were less than 20 per cent (table 22).

Table 22. Economic activity rates of persons aged 15 years and over by sex: 1976, 1981 and 1986 censuses

Census year	Economic activity rate (per cent)		
	Both sexes	Male	Female
1976	47.5	77.0	16.5
1981	47.2	78.5	14.6
1986	49.2	76.2	19.4

Source: Reports of the 1976, 1981 and 1986 censuses.

However, the underreporting of women's participation in economic activities was acknowledged in the report of the 1986 population census. Consequently, at the 1991 census, each person aged 10 years and over was asked a series of questions about activities during the week preceding the census and, on the basis of their responses, all persons were classified as either economically active or economically inactive. A special set of questions was posed to women who described themselves initially as housewives to ascertain their participation in economic activities. As a result, a significant number of women who were reported being involved in subsistence agriculture or household economic activities were classified as economically active.

In addition to changes in definitions and concepts, changes in the classifications of occupations of the employed population were also introduced into the 1991 census. The 1988 version of the International Standard Classification of Occupations (ISCO-88), which was adopted in the 1991 census, is skill-based and differs considerably from versions used in the earlier censuses. For all these reasons, the 1991 census data on economic activity are not strictly comparable with those from the past censuses. Hence, the analysis in this section will be limited only to the data from the 1991 Census.

2. Labour force participation

According to the 1991 census, nearly 40 per cent of females and 77 per cent of males aged 15 years and over were economically active or in the labour force (table 23). The 1991 female labour force participation rate is more than twice the rate reported by the 1986 census (19.4 per cent) and the reported increase between 1986 and 1991 has largely to be attributed to more realistic definition of economic activity used in the 1991 census. Nevertheless, the 1991 female labour force participation rate is considerably lower than the male participation rate. Thus, although the Samoan women have achieved equality with men in regard to access to education (see table 12), they appear to have limited employment opportunities.

The age-specific participation rates for males and females in 1991 are given in table 24 (also see figure 3). It will be noted that these rates are higher for males than for females at all ages and that they are at a peak at ages 20 to 54 years for both sexes. At these ages, almost all the males and a little more than half the females were reported being in the labour force. Participation rate for females almost equalled the male rate only at ages 25-29 years. At the older age group, 60-64 years, the male participation rate (76.4 per cent) was more than 12 times the female rate (6.3 per cent).

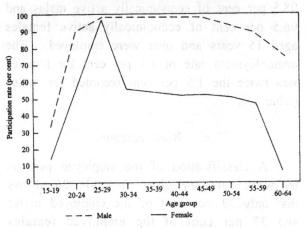

Figure 3. Age-specific labour force participation rates: 1991

Source: Report of the Census of Population and Housing, 1991.

Table 24. Labour force participation rate by age group and sex: 1991

Age group	Per cent in labour force	
	Male	Female
15-19	33.5	14.1
20-24	90.4	55.1
25-29	98.5	96.8
30-34	98.8	55.5
35-39	98.9	53.5
40-44	98.8	51.7
45-49	98.6	51.9
50-54	93.2	50.7
55-59	89.3	46.6
60-64	76.4	6.3

Source: Department of Statistics, *Report of the Census of Population and Housing, 1991.*

3. Employed persons

The economically active population or the labour force is defined to include the employed as well as the unemployed (those without employment but actively looking for work during

Table 23. Numerical and percentage distribution of persons aged 15 years and over by economic activity status and sex: 1991

Sex	Total		Economically active		Not economically active	
	Number	Per cent	Number	Per cent	Number	Per cent
Both sexes	95,829	100.0	57,142	59.6	38,687	40.4
Male	50,270	100.0	38,839	77.3	11,431	22.7
Female	45,559	100.0	18,303	40.2	27,256	59.8

Source: Department of Statistics, *Report of the Census of Population and Housing, 1991.*

23

the reference period of one week preceding the census). According to the 1991 census, 98.5 per cent of economically active males and 96.5 per cent of economically active females aged 15 years and over were employed. The unemployment rate of 3.1 per cent for females was twice the 1.5 per cent recorded for males (table 25).

a. Work category

A classification of the employed persons by work category given in table 26 shows that only 33 per cent of the employed males and 37 per cent of the employed females claimed to be either in paid work (worked primarily to earn money) or to have a paid job but not at work at the time of the census. The majority (67 per cent among males and 63 per cent among females) worked primarily to grow, gather or catch food.

b. Industrial attachment

Distribution of the employed persons by major industrial sector shows that the vast majority among males (72.7 per cent) as well as

females (66.4 per cent) were engaged in agriculture, forestry and fishing sector. The second largest employment sector was the major industrial group of community, social and personal services; a higher proportion among females (18.7 per cent) than males (10.5 per cent) was employed in this industrial sector. The third largest source of employment was wholesale and retail trade including hotels and restaurants for females (5.8 per cent), and construction sector for males (5.0 per cent). A higher proportion among females than among males was employed in mining and manufacturing and in finance, insurance and business sectors (table 27).

Although only 3.3 per cent of employed females are engaged in the mining and manufacturing sector, they constitute nearly 49 per cent of all persons employed in this industrial group. According to a 1989 survey conducted by the Department of Economic Development, 47 per cent of those engaged in manufacturing were concentrated in food, beverage and tobacco processing, while 23 per cent were found in wood products and furniture making.

Table 25. Classification of economically active persons aged 15 years and over by employment category and sex: 1991

Category	Both sexes		Male		Female	
	Number	Per cent	Number	Per cent	Number	Per cent
Employed	55,967	97.9	38,240	98.5	17,727	96.9
Unemployed	1,175	2.1	599	1.5	576	3.1
Economically active	57,142	100.0	38,839	100.0	18,303	100.0

Source: Department of Statistics, *Report of the Census of Population and Housing, 1991.*

Table 26. Numerical and percentage distribution of employed persons by work category and sex: 1991

Work category	Both sexes		Male		Female	
	Number	Per cent	Number	Per cent	Number	Per cent
Worked primarily to earn money	18,682	33.4	12,284	32.1	6,398	36.1
Had paid job but not at work	593	1.0	450	1.2	143	0.8
Worked primarily to grow, gather or catch food	36,692	65.6	25,506	66.7	11,186	63.1
Total	55,967	100.0	38,240	100.0	17,727	100.0

Source: Department of Statistics, *Report of the Census of Population and Housing, 1991.*

24

Table 27. Numerical and percentage distribution of employed persons by major industrial sector and sex: 1991

Major industrial sector	Both sexes		Male		Female	
	Number	Per cent	Number	Per cent	Number	Per cent
Agriculture, forestry, fishing	39,555	70.7	27,783	72.7	11,772	66.4
Mining and manufacturing	1,276	2.3	684	1.8	592	3.3
Electricity, gas and water	642	1.1	585	1.5	57	0.3
Construction	2,024	3.6	1,907	5.0	117	0.7
Wholesale and retail trade, restaurants and hotels	1,861	3.3	836	2.2	1,025	5.8
Transport, storage, communications	1,897	3.4	1,675	4.4	222	1.3
Finance, insurance, business services	1,370	2.4	744	1.9	626	3.5
Community, social, personal services	7,342	13.1	4,026	10.5	3,316	18.7
All sectors	55,967	100.0	38,240	100.0	17,727	100.0

Source: Department of Statistics, *Report of the Census of Population and Housing, 1991.*

A large number of women are also employed in other industries producing coconut products and garment making.

The distribution of the employed persons by primary, secondary and tertiary sectors shows that about 67 per cent of the females are employed in the primary sector; 4 per cent in the secondary and 29 per cent in the tertiary sectors. The corresponding proportions for males are 73 per cent, 8 per cent and 19 per cent respectively (table 28).

c. Occupational structure

The occupational distribution of the employed persons more or less reflects the pattern of distribution according to major industrial groups. As expected, a very high percentage of males (70.5 per cent) as well as females (64.4 per cent) were employed as agricultural

or fishing workers in 1991. The second largest proportion among males (15.5 per cent) was engaged in "other occupations", which include such jobs as plant and machine operators and assemblers and a range of manual and elementally occupations. In contrast, a significantly higher proportion of employed women (28.2 per cent) was employed as senior officials, professionals, technicians, clerks, as well as service, shop and sales workers (table 29).

d. Employment status

At the 1991 census, the employed persons were classified in terms of their employment status into four broad categories: employer, paid employee, self-employed and unpaid family workers. According to this census, the largest proportion of employed males (66.8 per cent) as well as employed females (65.0 per cent) were engaged as unpaid family workers. Paid

Table 28. Classification of employed persons by three broad industrial sector and sex: 1991

Broad sector	Both sexes		Male		Female	
	Number	Per cent	Number	Per cent	Number	Per cent
Primary	39,642	70.8	27,855	72.8	11,787	66.5
Secondary	3,855	6.9	3,104	8.1	751	4.2
Tertiary	12,470	22.3	7,281	19.1	5,189	29.3
Total	55,967	100.0	38,240	100.0	17,727	100.0

Source: Department of Statistics, *Report of the Census of Population and Housing, 1991.*

Table 29. Numerical and percentage distribution of employed persons by major occupational group and sex: 1991

Major occupational sector	Both sexes		Male		Female	
	Number	Per cent	Number	Per cent	Number	Per cent
Senior officials, professionals, technicians and clerks	7,779	13.9	4,111	10.8	3,668	20.7
Services, shop and market sales workers	2,558	4.6	1,222	3.2	1,336	7.5
Agriculture and fisheries workers	38,399	68.6	26,977	70.5	11,422	64.4
Other occupations	7,231	12.9	5,930	15.5	1,301	7.3
All occupations	55,967	100.0	38,240	100.0	17,727	100.0

Source: Department of Statistics, *Report of the Census of Population and Housing, 1991.*

employees constituted the second largest category with 26.0 per cent of employed males and 31.7 per cent of employed females. The proportion of those reported self-employed was considerably higher among males (5.9 per cent) than among females (2.1 per cent). The percentage of persons working as employers was nearly the same for males and females (table 30).

4. Unemployed persons

According to the 1991 census, there were 1,175 persons aged 15 years and over who were reported unemployed; that is, they did not work during the reference week but claimed that they were looking for and were available for work. Out of the total of unemployed persons, 599 or about 51 per cent were males and 576 or 49 per cent were females. The unemployed persons constituted 2.1 per cent of all persons classified as economically active; this proportion for females (3.1 per cent) was twice the proportion for males (see table 25).

While the overall unemployment rate of 2.1 per cent of the economically active persons may not be high, compared with most Pacific island countries, analysis by age and sex reveals considerable concentration among the young. The unemployment rate of 6.2 per cent for all persons aged 15-19 years is almost three times the overall rate of 2.1 per cent. The second highest unemployment rate, 5.5 per cent, is in respect of persons aged 20-24 years (table 31).

It is also clear from table 31 that unemployment among females is higher than among males; at almost all ages, the female rates are nearly the same as the corresponding male rates. Amongst young females aged 15-19 years, the 1991 unemployment rate was 11.3 per cent and the corresponding male rate was 6.2 per cent. At ages 20-24 years, 8.8 per cent of females as against 6.5 per cent of the economically active males were unemployed. Thus, unemployment appears to be a relatively

Table 30. Classification of employed persons by employment status and sex: 1991

Employment status	Both sexes		Male		Female	
	Number	Per cent	Number	Per cent	Number	Per cent
Employers	700	1.3	490	1.3	210	1.2
Paid employees	15,566	27.8	9,949	26.0	5,617	31.7
Self-employed	2,633	4.7	2,256	5.9	377	2.1
Unpaid family workers	37,068	66.2	25,545	66.8	11,523	65.0
All statuses	55,967	100.0	38,240	100.0	17,727	100.0

Source: Department of Statistics, *Report of the Census of Population and Housing, 1991.*

Table 31. Unemployment rates by age and sex: 1991

(per cent)

Age group	Both sexes	Male	Female
15-19	6.2	4.4	11.3
20-24	5.5	4.2	8.8
25-29	1.3	0.9	2.0
30-34	0.6	0.5	0.8
35-39	0.4	0.4	0.5
40-44	0.3	0.2	0.5
45-49	0.1	0.1	0.2
50+	0.1	0.1	0.2
All ages 15+	2.1	1.5	3.1

Source: Report of the Census of Population and Housing, 1991.

more serious problem among the youth, particularly females. This highlights the difficulties that young females have in finding suitable employment.

5. Women in agriculture

The 1989 Census of Agriculture revealed many significant differences between men and women in terms of being operators of agricultural land, number of hours worked and the capacity in which they were engaged. The census defined an operator as a person who exercises management control over the operation of the agricultural holding. Since the holding was operated by a single household, the head of that household was, in most cases, the operator. There could be more than one operators per holding.

According to the Agriculture Census, females constituted only 2.4 per cent of operators in the country, 2.2 per cent in the rural and 4.6 per cent in the urban areas. Male operators spent an average of 99 hours per month in agriculture, while their female counterparts spent on an average of 82 hours. Both males and females spent fewer hours in agriculture in urban compared with rural areas (table 32).

A total of 4,664 women were engaged as unpaid workers and they constituted 27 per cent of all unpaid workers in agriculture. About 27 per cent of the female unpaid workers were 40 years old and over, while the corresponding proportion among males was only 14 per cent. More than 80 per cent of both male and female unpaid workers had no paid job; 12 per cent among males and 6 per cent among females had a full-time job. In the urban areas, 38 per cent of male and 22 per cent of female unpaid agricultural workers had a full-time job; the corresponding proportions in Savaii were 7 per cent and 4 per cent respectively (see annex table E.1). While in Apia women with full-time as well as with part-time paid jobs spent an equal number of hours as unpaid labour, in the Rest of Upolu those with a part-time job spent more hours in agriculture, compared with those with no paid job.

The 1989 Agricultural Census also showed that only 8 per cent of all agricultural workers were paid labour and that females constituted only 6 per cent of all paid workers. About 15

Table 32. Average number of hours worked per month by agricultural operators and unpaid agricultural workers, by sex and residence: 1989

Residence/region	Agricultural operators		Paid job status of unpaid agricultural workers							
			Total		Full-time		Part-time		None	
	Male	Female	Male	Female	Male	Female	Male	Female	Male	Female
Apia urban area	83	66	67	59	47	35	56	35	82	66
North West Upolu	98	83	70	59	44	29	70	53	75	62
Rest of Upolu	103	86	77	66	55	35	64	77	82	68
Savaii	100	84	54	64	57	48	64	54	84	66
Upolu	99	81	70	63	51	33	65	70	80	65
Samoa	99	82	63	64	52	38	65	63	81	65

Source: Department of Statistics and Department of Agriculture, Report on the Census of Agriculture, 1989.

per cent of male and 12 per cent of female paid agricultural workers were aged 15-19 years, while 8 per cent of males and 20 per cent of the females were aged 40 years and over.

6. Informal sector employment

A manifestation of the tight labour market situation in Samoa is the growing urban informal sector around the main markets in Apia. Lack of remunerative employment opportunities, poor cash earnings by family labour and a growing feeling of independence among rural youths cause rural people to migrate to and around Apia urban area. An increasing number of these migrants are setting up their own business on pavements and roadside areas. Some more affluent among them have already put up small wooden shops along the seaside, opposite the main market. These vendors and small shop owners are often helped by their family members in their business activities. An estimated 600 households were engaged in such activities in 1991 and this number was then estimated to increase by 10 per cent annually.

A small survey of randomly selected vendors was conducted in 1991 to obtain information about the characteristics of informal sector entrepreneurs. This survey, conducted with the assistance of Labour Department officials, focused on three main activities: selling of vegetables, fruits and root crops, selling of handicraft items, and selling of imported commodities such as ready made garments, perfumes, foot wears etc.

The survey revealed that more females than males were engaged in urban informal economic activities and that most of these entrepreneurs were above 30 years of age. Those who sold vegetables did more business than others and most of the agricultural products were self-grown. Imported items were generally supplied by relatives and friends residing abroad; supplies of these goods were also available from American Samoa and Hawaii. Those selling perishable items spent more hours a day than those dealing in non-perishable commodities. Most of these entrepreneurs consi-

dered financial assistance a major help to expand their business.

7. Private sector employment

The total private sector workforce was estimated at 12,592 during the last quarter of 1991 and of this number 41 per cent were women. Returns obtained from establishments also indicate that females constituted 22 per cent of all private sector employees in the primary sector and 43 per cent in the secondary and tertiary sectors. A recently established Yasaki, a factory assembling electrical car parts for export, reported a total workforce during the last quarter of 1992 of 590 persons of whom 575 or 97.4 per cent were females.

8. Women in business

In 1991, a total of 2,862 private sector employers were registered with the National Provident Fund; only 148 or 5.2 per cent of these employers were women. The female employers were engaged in various types of activities such as retail and wholesale trade, restaurant/accommodation, transport hire and services, manufacturing of food and clothing etc.

The Women in Business Foundation was established in 1991 with the main objective of promoting the interests of women in business. The membership of this foundation has been increasing over the years and women committees are now part of this foundation. The activities of the foundation include organizing displays at public functions and erecting stalls to enable women to sell their products and handicrafts.

Public functions provide the most important outlet for small food traders. In 1990-1991, nearly 49 per cent of the food stalls operating in Apia Park were run by women, 44 per cent by men and the remaining 7 per cent by companies or clubs.

9. Access to credit facilities

In July 1991, the Development Bank of Samoa approved 7,782 current loans of which 713 or 9.2 per cent were granted to women individually or jointly. Nearly 85 per cent of loans to individual women were for agriculture, and nearly 47 per cent of these loans were classified as "large" (see annex table E.2).

A small-scale survey of women in agriculture found that 26 per cent of families in Upolu and 18 per cent of families in Savaii had applied for loans for agricultural purposes. Among these applicants, 77 per cent in Upolu and 55 per cent in Savaii were successful in obtaining the loans.

In 1989, the United Nations Development Programme (UNDP) made funds available to two women's groups, one to finance training for urban women in handicraft production and the other to training in sewing machine repair and dressmaking for unemployed rural women. In 1990, the UNDP granted loans to four women's groups for projects such as development of pig sties, cattle raising, reconstruction of a spring pool and construction of cement gallon stoves.

In 1991, the South Pacific Commission, under its Small Grants Scheme, granted a sum of US$ 5,000 to the Ministry of Women's Affairs to set up a revolving scheme. The purpose of this revolving scheme is to enable individual women as well as women's groups to borrow money at very low interest rates to start small development projects within the vicinity of their homes or for community projects.

10. Not economically active persons

As noted earlier (table 23), in 1991 there were 38,687 persons aged 15 years and over who were reported not economically active.

Of these, 11,431 or 29.5 per cent were males and 27,256 or 70.5 per cent were females. The numerical distribution of the not economically active persons by age group, sex and kind of activity pursued is given in annex table E.3.

It will be noted from annex table E.3 that the kind of activity pursued by persons who have been classified as not economically active is, by and large, a function of age and sex. Although the largest proportion (41.2 per cent) of all not economically persons were engaged in full-time education, this proportion varied markedly between the two sexes; the proportion of males (72.0 per cent) was about two and a half times that of females (28.3 per cent). Similarly, about 53.0 per cent of females as against only 1.6 per cent of males who were not economically active were engaged in household or domestic chores (also see table 33).

Nearly 88 per cent of males and 90 per cent of females reporting full-time education as the reason for being not economically active were aged 15-19 years. Similarly, 93 per cent of females reporting being engaged in household chores were aged 20 years and over. The "other" group of activity, which mainly includes retired persons, naturally focuses on elderly persons; nearly 87 per cent of the males and 94 per cent of the females under this category were 60 years and over in age.

F. WOMEN IN PUBLIC LIFE

The participation of women in decision-making processes at various levels is not only a major indicator of their status in society, but

Table 33. Numerical and percentage distribution of not economically active persons by kind of activity pursued and sex: 1991

Activity	Both sexes		Male		Female	
	Number	Per cent	Number	Per cent	Number	Per cent
Full-time education	15,948	41.2	8,226	72.0	7,722	28.3
Household duties	14,591	37.7	186	1.6	14,405	52.9
Other	8,148	21.1	3,019	26.4	5,129	18.8
Total	38,687	100.0	11,431	100.0	27,256	100.0

Source: Department of Statistics, *Report of the Census of Population and Housing, 1991.*

also an important means for enhancing their socio-economic advancement and contribution. In Samoa, the recognition in recent years of the crucial role that women could play in the public life of the country has resulted in slow but gradual increase in the number of women appointed or elected to decision-making positions in both political and public offices.

1. Women as voters

Since independence in 1962, only the *matai* were eligible to vote at various elections at the national and local level. However, with the introduction in 1990 of universal suffrage, all males and females aged 21 years and over were granted the voting right and for the first time this right came to be exercised at the general elections held in 1991.

In spite of the granting of universal suffrage, women remain marginalized in political decision-making processes, because only the *matai* are eligible to stand as candidates for various elections and there are only a very few women who hold *matai* titles. Further, information is not available as to the percentage of women aged 21 years and over who have either registered themselves as voters or have actually exercised their voting right. It is, however, estimated that about 40 per cent of the people aged 21 years and over actually vote.

2. Women in parliament

As noted earlier in Section B, the Parliament of Samoa now comprises 49 members of whom two are elected by citizens by European extraction from a separate roll. The first woman member of Parliament was elected in 1970 and she was also appointed as Deputy Speaker in the same year. Currently, there are two women *matai* elected as members of Parliament, one of whom is Minister of Education and the first woman minister ever in the country. It is also interesting to note that women representatives are always returned by the same constituencies, although it is not always the same person who is returned.

3. Women in local government

In terms of the provisions of the Pulenuu Act enacted by the Parliament, the village *pulenuu* are selected from their respective villages to serve in office for a three-year term. The selection of *pulenuu*, whether male or female, is based on the decision of the respective village councils and is restricted only to *matai* of the village. In 1994, there were 229 *pulenuu* of whom only one was a woman from the village of Falefa in Upolu. In previous years, three women were selected to this position from three different villages.

4. Women in administrative and executive positions

In 1990, there were 3,777 public service employees in the country of whom 2002 or 53 per cent were females. About 43 per cent of all female employees were less than 30 years of age, while the corresponding proportion of males was 36 per cent. In the same year, 12 per cent of female public servants were aged 50 years, compared with 18 per cent among males. In 1992, women again constituted 53 per cent of the 3,861 pulic servants. By and large, women are concentrated at the lower levels of the service; only 11 per cent among females compared to 27 per cent among males were at the salary scale of 10,000 *tala* and over.

In 1992, there were 1,289 public servants in administrative grades, of whom 681 or 53 per cent were females. Although women constituted a significantly higher proportion of officers in the administrative grades, they were mostly concentrated at the lower levels of these grades. As many as 514 or 75 per cent of the 681 female public servants in administrative grades were serving in the lower grades 1 to 6; the corresponding proportion among males was 59 per cent. Only 9.4 per cent among females compared with 24.0 per cent among males were in grade 10 and above. Also, there were only 6 women, compared to 36 men, serving as heads or deputies (table 34).

Table 34. Public servants in administrative grades by grade and sex: 1 January 1992

Grade	Both sexes		Male		Female		Per cent female
	Number	Per cent	Number	Per cent	Number	Per cent	
1.	428	33.2	134	22.0	294	43.2	68.7
2.	57	4.4	22	3.6	35	5.1	61.4
3.	111	8.6	61	10.0	50	7.3	45.0
4.	67	5.2	32	5.3	35	5.1	52.2
5.	100	7.8	60	9.9	40	5.9	40.0
6.	108	8.4	48	7.9	60	8.8	55.6
7.	62	4.8	36	5.9	26	3.8	41.9
8.	85	6.6	44	7.2	41	6.0	48.2
9.	60	4.7	24	3.9	36	5.3	60.0
10.	47	3.6	28	4.6	19	2.8	40.4
11.	27	2.1	16	2.6	11	1.6	40.7
12.	36	2.8	24	3.9	12	1.8	33.3
13.	26	2.0	20	3.3	6	0.9	23.1
14.	26	2.0	17	2.8	9	1.3	34.6
Special grade	4	0.3	3	0.5	1	0.1	25.0
Deputy[a/]	22	1.7	18	3.0	4	0.6	18.2
Head[b/]	23	1.8	21	3.5	2	0.3	8.7
All grades	1,289	100.0	608	100.0	681	100.0	52.8

Source: Public Service Commission.

Note: [a/] Deputy Head of Department.
[b/] Head of Department.

At the end of 1994, there were five female executive heads of government departments: Ministry of Women Affairs, Lands and Environment, Legislative Assembly, Lands and Titles Court and the Department of Tourism. In addition, the Deputy Commissioner of Inland Revenue and the Deputy Controller and Chief Auditor were women. In Samoa, women also hold positions as Assistant Director (Planning and Research) of Education and the Head of the Health Planning and Information Unit in the Department of Health, Assistant Secretary to Economic and Aid Division and Assistant Secretary (Scholarship Division) in the Ministry of Foreign Affairs.

In 1994, for the first time a woman was elected to the position of a judge to serve in the Lands and Titles Court. In that year, a woman was also elected for the first time as Director of the Public Service Association. Although a recent decision by the Cabinet stipulates that women should be included as members of semi-government boards and corporations, only less than 10 per cent of the members of more than 50 Boards and Committees are women.

Samoa has two High Commissions (one in Wellington, New Zealand, and the other in Canberra, Australia) and two Embassies (one in Brussels, Belgium, and the other in New York). Among the diplomatic outpostings, one woman serves as High Commissioner, one as First Secretary and one as Second Secretary. Although women in the past served as First and Second Secretaries, the present woman High Commissioner based in Wellington is the first woman ever holding such a position, which is usually a political appointment.

PART II:
ANNEX STATISTICAL TABLES

Table B.1 Prevalence of hypertension, obesity and diabetes by sex and urban/rural residence: 1978 and 1991[a]

Disease/sex	Urban area			Rural area					
	Apia			Poutasi			Tuasivi		
	1978	1991	Percentage increase	1978	1991	Percentage increase	1978	1991	Percentage increase
Male									
Hypertension	12.7	15.1	19	2.2	3.0	36	6.2	7.3	18
Obesity	17.2	31.9	85	7.4	20.0	170	3.3	15.9	382
Diabetes	10.0	11.9	19	0.7	6.4	814	3.4	9.0	165
Female									
Hypertension	19.5	16.0	(18)[b]	6.9	7.6	10	7.1	4.5	(37)[b]
Obesity	14.6	22.4	53	7.7	14.0	82	3.2	13.9	334
Diabetes	10.3	18.0	75	5.5	6.0	9	6.0	9.4	57

Source: World Bank, *Health Priorities and Options in the World Bank's Pacific Member Countries*, Report No. 11620-EAP, October 1994.

Notes: [a] Comparison of prevalence of hypertension (BP > 160), and obesity (weight > 100 kg), and diabetes (2 hour post 75g plasma glucose > 11 mmol/1 or subject on insulin or oral hypoglycemic therapy), and per cent change in each survey area.

[b] ( ) Represents decrease.

Table C.1 Numerical distribution of enumerated population by five-year age group and sex: 1976, 1981, 1986 and 1991 censuses

	1976			1981			1986			1991		
	Both sexes	Male	Fe-male	Both sexes	Male	Fe-male	Both sexes	Male	Fe-male	Both sexes	Male	Fe-male
0-4	24,646	12,995	11,651	22,866	12,095	10,771	22,109	11,898	10,211	23,245	12,076	11,169
5-9	24,973	13,125	11,848	22,848	11,991	10,857	21,023	11,273	9,750	21,177	11,169	10,008
10-14	23,627	12,220	11,407	23,525	12,438	11,087	21,713	11,733	9,980	21,047	11,086	9,961
15-19	19,552	10,398	9,154	20,896	10,919	9,977	21,137	11,479	9,658	20,280	10,999	9,281
20-24	12,049	6,457	5,592	15,000	7,868	7,132	15,797	8,502	7,295	15,647	8,707	6,940
25-29	7,881	3,892	3,989	9,673	4,968	4,705	11,563	6,040	5,523	12,374	6,585	5,789
30-34	6,685	3,294	3,391	6,862	3,412	3,450	8,617	4,385	4,232	9,927	5,155	4,772
35-39	6,676	3,321	3,355	6,165	3,043	3,122	6,365	3,172	3,193	7,643	3,874	3,769
40-44	5,790	2,885	2,905	6,000	2,986	3,014	5,929	2,953	2,976	6,009	3,015	2,994
45-49	5,302	2,647	2,655	5,158	2,564	2,594	5,396	2,722	2,674	5,180	2,586	2,594
50-54	4,530	2,294	2,236	4,895	2,476	2,419	4,891	2,510	2,381	4,880	2,437	2,443
55-59	3,360	1,732	1,628	3,955	2,087	1,868	4,083	2,151	1,932	4,089	2,096	1,993
60-64	2,415	1,240	1,175	2,880	1,459	1,421	3,391	1,805	1,586	3,452	1,730	1,722
65-69	1,715	871	844	1,876	944	932	2,160	1,169	991	2,987	1,537	1,450
70-74	1,188	593	595	1,242	605	637	1,415	724	691	1,661	801	860
75+	1,594	675	919	1,618	678	940	1,782	839	943	1,700	748	952
Not stated	–	–	–	890	494	396	37	15	22	–	–	–
All ages	151,983	78,639	73,344	156,349	81,027	75,322	157,408	83,370	74,038	161,298	84,601	76,697

Source: Department of Statistics.

Table C.2 Percentage distribution of enumerated population by five-year age group and sex: 1976, 1981, 1986 and 1991 censuses

	1976			1981			1986			1991		
	Both sexes	Male	Fe-male	Both sexes	Male	Fe-male	Both sexes	Male	Fe-male	Both sexes	Male	Fe-male
0-4	16.2	16.5	15.9	14.6	14.9	14.3	14.0	14.3	13.8	14.4	14.3	14.6
5-9	16.4	16.7	16.2	14.6	14.8	14.4	13.4	13.5	13.2	13.1	13.2	13.0
10-14	15.5	15.5	15.6	15.0	15.4	14.7	13.8	14.1	13.5	13.0	13.1	13.0
15-19	12.9	13.2	12.5	13.4	13.5	13.2	13.4	13.8	13.0	12.6	13.0	12.1
20-24	7.9	8.2	7.6	9.6	9.7	9.5	10.0	10.2	9.9	9.7	10.3	9.0
25-29	5.2	4.9	5.4	6.2	6.1	6.2	7.3	7.2	7.5	7.7	7.8	7.5
30-34	4.4	4.2	4.6	4.4	4.2	4.6	5.5	5.3	5.7	6.2	6.1	6.2
35-39	4.4	4.2	4.6	3.9	3.8	4.1	4.0	3.8	4.3	4.7	4.6	4.9
40-44	3.8	3.7	4.0	3.8	3.7	4.0	3.8	3.5	4.0	3.7	3.6	3.9
45-49	3.5	3.4	3.6	3.3	3.2	3.4	3.4	3.3	3.6	3.2	3.1	3.4
50-54	3.0	2.9	3.0	3.1	3.1	3.2	3.1	3.0	3.2	3.0	2.9	3.2
55-59	2.2	2.2	2.2	2.5	2.6	2.5	2.6	2.6	2.6	2.5	2.5	2.6
60-64	1.6	1.6	1.6	1.8	1.8	1.9	2.2	2.2	2.1	2.1	2.0	2.2
65-69	1.1	1.1	1.2	1.2	1.2	1.2	1.4	1.4	1.3	1.9	1.8	1.9
70-74	0.8	0.8	0.8	0.8	0.7	0.8	0.9	0.9	0.9	1.0	0.9	1.1
75+	1.0	0.9	1.3	1.0	0.8	1.2	1.1	1.0	1.3	1.1	0.9	1.2
Not stated	–	–	–	0.6	0.6	0.5	–	–	–	–	–	–
All ages	100.0	100.0	100.0	100.0	100.0	100.0	100.0	100.0	100.0	100.0	100.0	100.0

Source: Department of Statistics.

Table C.3 Population and school enrolments by age group and sex: 1971, 1976, 1981 and 1986 censuses

Year and age group	Population			School enrolments		
	Both sexes	Male	Female	Both sexes	Male	Female
1971						
5-9	24,918	12,908	12,010	18,337	9,429	8,908
10-14	22,154	11,704	10,450	20,473	10,573	9,900
15-19	17,137	9,144	7,993	7,507	3,757	3,750
5-19	64,209	33,756	30,453	46,317	23,759	22,558
1976						
5-9	24,973	13,125	11,848	20,470	10,782	9,688
10-14	23,627	12,220	11,407	22,323	11,365	10,958
15-19	19,552	10,398	9,154	10,533	5,157	5,376
5-19	68,152	35,743	32,409	53,326	27,304	26,022
1981						
5-9	22,848	11,991	10,857	18,526	9,666	8,860
10-14	23,525	12,438	11,087	22,933	12,013	10,920
15-19	20,896	10,919	9,977	13,571	6,621	6,950
5-19	67,269	35,348	31,921	55,030	28,300	26,730
1986						
5-9	21,023	11,273	9,750	18,576	9,787	8,789
10-14	21,713	11,733	9,980	17,650	8,957	8,693
15-19	21,137	11,479	9,658	15,714	7,870	7,844
5-19	63,873	34,485	29,388	51,940	26,614	25,326

Source: Department of Statistics and Department of Education.

Table D.1 Number of hospital and community reported births: 1988 to 1992

Year	All births		National hospital[a]		District hospitals[b]		Community (TBAs)[c]	
	Number	Per cent	Number	Per cent	Number	Per cent	Number	Per cent
1988	4,611	100.0	1,998	43.3	1,502	32.6	1,111	24.1
1989	4,589	100.0	1,991	43.4	1,426	31.1	1,172	25.5
1990	4,503	100.0	2,028	45.0	1,380	30.6	1,095	24.3
1991	4,937	100.0	2,132	43.2	1,618	32.8	1,187	24.0
1992	4,196	100.0	2,408	57.4	928	22.1	860	20.5

Source: Department of Health. Annual Report 1991 and 1992.

Note:
[a] National hospital is located in Apia.
[b] There are 13 district hospitals of which 7 are in rural Upolu and 6 are in Savaii.
[c] Community births are usually attended to by traditional birth attendants (TBAs).

Table E.1 Percentage of persons working in an unpaid capacity by paid job status, sex and residence: 1989

Sex/residence	Paid job status			
	Total	Full-time	Part-time	None
Male				
Apia Urban area	100	38	7	55
North West Upolu	100	13	11	76
Rest of Upolu	100	12	7	81
Savaii	100	7	6	87
Upolu	100	15	8	77
Samoa	100	11	7	82
Female				
Apia Urban area	100	22	2	76
North West Upolu	100	7	4	88
Rest of Upolu	100	7	8	85
Savaii	100	4	6	90
Upolu	100	8	6	85
Samoa	100	6	6	88

Source: Department of Statistics, and Department of Agriculture, *Report on the 1989 Census of Agriculture.*

Table E.2 Current loans to women by the Development Bank of Samoa by purpose of loans: July 1991

Purpose of loan	Individual	Joint[a]	Committee
Agriculture-large	303	33	0
Agriculture-small	251	9	0
Industries	59	8	0
Cocoa suspensory	22	3	0
IFAD[b]	8	0	0
Group	3	0	0
Infrastructure	5	0	0
Women's activities	0	0	9
Total	651	53	9

Source: Development Bank of Western Samoa.

Note: [a] Loans granted to husband and wife jointly.
[b] IFAD loans use money from International Fund for Agricultural Development.

Table E.3 Distribution of the "not economically active" persons by age group, type of activity pursued and sex: 1991

Age group	Total		Full-time education		Household duties		Other	
	Male	Female	Male	Female	Male	Female	Male	Female
15-19	7,309	7,970	7,273	6,987	–	961	36	22
20-24	840	3,118	799	622	–	2,470	41	26
25-29	97	2,502	69	48	–	2,424	28	30
30-34	61	2,121	46	35	–	2,075	15	11
35-39	44	1,751	22	15	–	1,720	22	16
40-44	36	1,447	8	5	–	1,421	28	21
45-49	37	1,248	2	4	–	1,224	35	20
50-54	166	1,204	2	–	87	1,154	77	50
55-59	225	1,065	2	4	99	956	124	105
60-64	411	1,613	3	–	–	–	408	1,613
65+	2,205	3,217	–	2	–	–	2,205	3,215
All ages	11,431	27,256	8,226	7,722	186	14,405	3,019	5,129

Source: Department of Statistics, *Report of the Census of Population and Housing, 1991.*

REFERENCES

Asian Development Bank, *Asian Development Outlook, 1995.*

Central Bank, *Annual Report for 1990 (Apia, 1990).*

Central Bank, *Annual Report for 1993 (Apia, 1993).*

Department of Agriculture and Ministry of Womens Affairs, *Report on Women in Agriculture Survey: Summary (Apia, 1993).*

Department of Economic Development, *Western Samoa's Sixth Development Plan 1988-1990* (Apia, December 1987).

Department of Health, *Annual Report, 1988-1990.*

Department of Health, *Annual Report, 1991 and 1992.*

Department of Labour, *Report on the Employment Situation in the Private Sector for the Fourth Quarter (October-December) 1991* (Apia, 9 July 1992).

Department of Statistics and Department of Agriculture, *Report on the 1989 Census of Agriculture.*

Department of Statistics, *Migration Dataset* (Apia, 1990-1992).

Department of Statistics, *Report of the Census of Population and Housing, 1991.*

Department of Statistics, *Annual Statistical Abstract, 1991.*

Fairburn, T.I.J., *Island Economies.* Institute of Pacific Studies, University of South Pacific (Suva, 1985).

Public Service Commission, *List of Persons Employed on the Permanent and Temporary Staff of Western Samoa Public Service as at 1 January 1992* (Apia, 1992).

Rosali Miles *et al., Employment in Western Samoa: Present and Potential.* ILO/UNDP/AIDAB. Employment Promotion, Manpower Planning and Labour Administration in the Pacific (March 1992) Draft

Shankman P., "The effects of migration and remittances on Western Samoa" in Mapherson, C.B. Shore and R. Franco (eds.). *New Neighbours: Islanders in Adaptation* (Santa Cruz, University of California, 1978).

Sio, B., *Western Samoa Country Statement.* Paper presented to the Conference on the Effects of Urbanization and Western Diet on the Health of Pacific Island Populations (Suva, 1981). Unpublished.

South Pacific Commission, *Population Statistics.* Statistical Bulletin No. 42 (Noumea, 1995).

United Nations, *World Population Prospects: The 1994 Revision.* Department for Economic and Social Information and Policy Analysis. New York 1995.

Western Samoa Public Service. Association, Handbook for WSPSA Member, 1992.

World Bank, *Health Priorities and Options in the World Bank's Pacific Member Countries,* Report No. 11620-EAP (Washington D.C., October 1994).